SUNDERLAND
VOLUNTEER LIFE BRIGADE

By kind permission of Anne Williams and John Dale.

SUNDERLAND
VOLUNTEER LIFE BRIGADE

Kathleen Gill

The
History
Press

To the members of Sunderland Volunteer Life Brigade, past and present, who have dedicated over 130 years of service to saving life, and to all those who risk their own lives in rescuing others from the dangers of the sea.

First published 2010

The History Press
The Mill, Brimscombe Port
Stroud, Gloucestershire, GL5 2QG
www.thehistorypress.co.uk

© Kathleen Gill, 2010

The right of Kathleen Gill to be identified as the Author
of this work has been asserted in accordance with the
Copyrights, Designs and Patents Act 1988.

British Library Cataloguing in Publication Data.
A catalogue record for this book is available from the British Library.

ISBN 978 0 7524 5091 9

Typesetting and origination by The History Press
Printed in Great Britain
Manufacturing managed by Jellyfish Print Solutions Ltd

CONTENTS

FOREWORD

The rescue of those in peril on the sea has always been a cause dear to Wearsiders, with their long tradition of seafaring, and this book provides a fitting tribute to the selfless devotion of members of the Sunderland Volunteer Life Brigade, founded in the nineteenth century when going to sea was the most dangerous job of all. Tempestuous seas left this treacherous stretch of the north-east coastline littered with wrecks and crews in mortal danger – in the Great Storm of 1911, for example, forty ships and 200 lives were lost.

However, this is much more than a book about rescues. The sense of close-knit community is captured by Kathleen Gill, even to naming neighbouring streets in which brigadesmen lived, and describing how Captain Wellburn of the brigade knocked on doors in the hard times of 1927 to ask for – and to receive – food for a crew of seventeen, sheltering, cold and hungry, in the VLB watch house, after being rescued one by one by breeches buoy when their ship, the *Efos*, went aground after rounding Roker Pier.

A chapter is devoted to a picture of the local economy, but the busy life of port and harbour in days gone by is also caught by passing references to the cargoes being carried by stricken ships: a Norwegian brigantine carrying pit props went aground on the North Sands in 1884; in the gales of 1919 the steamer *Solo*, carrying coal out of the Wear, collided with the Confield, bringing in esparto grass and iron ore; in 1940 the SS *Cairnglen*, with a precious wartime cargo of butter, bacon, wheat, engines and tyres, survived the long and dangerous voyage from Montreal only to come to grief on a reef at Marsden. There was never a shortage of volunteers to go to the rescue.

There are vivid descriptions of rescues and rescuers, even down to the difficulties of coping with heavy thick-knit ganseys whatever the weather in the days before the lightweight safety clothing of brigadesmen on their search and rescue duties today. Tales of gallantry abound, right up to the last breeches buoy rescue of 1963, when huge waves drove the *Adelfotis II* onto the beach at South Shields. With tugs and lifeboats unable to get near, the crew of twenty-three and the ship's small dog were rescued by the VLB, with brigadesmen acting as human anchors to prevent gear being blown out of the ground, and some going into the sea tied to safety lines when rescue lines to the breeches buoy became submerged.

In the greatest marathon of all, in October 1940 brigadesmen rescued the crews of the destroyers *Ashanti* and *Fame*, aground on rocks at Whitburn. A world record of 272 men were rescued, eighty-six by South Shields VLB and 186 by Sunderland. Those brigadesmen were on duty for thirty-two hours, braving mines, barbed wire and wartime blackout, as well as their accustomed battle with the sea. And still they were ready for another major rescue a few days later. At last there is a published account of their bravery.

Carol Roberton

ACKNOWLEDGEMENTS

I would like to thank the following for their help in the preparation of this book: my husband Ian, for his patience, encouragement and support, as well as many hours of proof reading; the directors, officers and members of Sunderland Volunteer Life Brigade, whose continuing service to those who use the coastal area around Sunderland inspired this book and who have supported this venture by allowing full access to all documents, records and photographs; Tynemouth Volunteer Life Brigade, for providing additional information; Sunderland Antiquarian Society for providing photographs from their archive.

The following institutions have also been very helpful: the Local Studies Section, Sunderland City Council Library, whose staff looked up references and sought sources as well as providing advice; the *Sunderland Echo*, for photographic material; The War Graves Photographic Project; North Tyneside Council Local Studies Service; Helston Museum, Cornwall, for pictures relating to Henry Trengrouse; the Tyne and Wear Archive Service, whose staff assisted with research into the records of the River Wear Commissioners; Cumbria Record Office for information on the Whitehaven Brigade.

My thanks also go to Anne Williams and John Dale, descendants of Captain John Herring, for allowing the use of the Herring sketches; Howard Glansfield, for the picture of his ancestor, John Leviss; Carol Roberton, for kindly agreeing to write the foreword; staff at The History Press, particularly Amy Rigg and Jennifer Younger, for their advice, help and encouragement to a first-time author.

INTRODUCTION

Great Britain, as an island nation, has a long and interesting history of maritime enterprise. The British people have relied on the sea for defence and on the shipping trade for the transportation of goods and passengers. By the mid-nineteenth century Great Britain had the largest merchant fleet in the world, and the coastal and Baltic trades from the north-east ports formed a large part of the traffic around the British coast. Each gale that blew, however, saw hundreds of men drowned, and from 1850 to 1865 approximately 20,000 vessels were lost around the British coast with huge loss of life. The late eighteenth and early nineteenth centuries were the periods when the hazards experienced by seagoing men and the loss of life, ships and cargoes began to become an area of concern for those involved in the shipping-related industries.

There was little regulation about the standard of ships, the training of ships' masters or of the loading of cargoes, and no organised means to attempt to rescue those seamen who were shipwrecked on the shores around the coast. The concerns about the conditions of seamen, and large-scale unemployment in the industry around this time, led to the founding of national societies dedicated to improving the lot of the sailor and his family. The British Sailors' Society was set up in 1818; the Sailors' Children's Society was founded in 1821 in Hull, and the Merchant Seamen's Orphan Asylum movement was established in 1827.

By 1843 Parliament had to appoint a Committee of Enquiry due to the large loss of life in January that year, when 240 ships and 500 lives were lost within three days. The lack of effective legislation left seamen largely unprotected and efforts to provide a safer working environment, and rescue services when disasters occurred, often fell to the efforts of philanthropists and local people.

The establishment of the Volunteer Life Brigade (VLB) movement is an illustration of one of the ways in which ordinary working men, along with local industrialists and businessmen, saw a need for action and then gave freely of their time and money to put necessary services into place. Many also put their own lives at risk to assist those coming to grief on the treacherous north-eastern coastline. The VLBs used shore-based apparatus when rescuing people from ships in danger; their work complemented that of lifeboat men, and they worked under the direction of HM Coastguard.

Sunderland VLB was one of hundreds of brigades set up and run by local people in order to help diminish the appalling loss of life around the British coast. It remains now as one of the three surviving VLBs in the country, all of which are based on the north-east coast, and continues to provide services to those who use the port of Sunderland; its harbour and its beaches. This is the story of the people who endeavoured to set up a VLB in Sunderland, of those who volunteered for service and supported its work. It describes some of the many rescues undertaken and the way in which the brigade has developed to provide a modern-day service.

one

THE DEVELOPMENT OF LIFESAVING AND FORMATION OF VOLUNTEER LIFE BRIGADES

Developments in lifesaving from the sea began in the late 1790s with the setting up of private lifeboats, and by the early 1800s technology had developed that enabled the use of mortars or rockets to assist in lifesaving, by getting a line onto stranded ships. It was within this context that the VLB movement was set up, the brigade at Sunderland having responsibility for one of the busiest and most treacherous stretches of coast. Shore-based lifesaving apparatus used in the case of shipwreck was available from the early 1800s and the development of apparatus took place in several areas of the country around this time.

One of these pioneers was Captain George William Manby (1766 – 1854) who witnessed the wreck of the gun brig *Snipe* off the coast at Yarmouth in 1807. Sixty lives were lost, including many women and children, on a wreck that took place just 50yds from the shore. Manby decided to try to devise a means of getting a line to ships to enable crew and passengers to be taken off. He experimented with firing a light line, by means of a mortar, which could then be used to put a heavier line onto a ship. Once secured this could then be used with a cradle or boat to rescue the crew.[1]

The apparatus was first used successfully in February 1808 when the brig *Elizabeth* foundered off Yarmouth and the crew of seven were saved. In 1810 Manby's mortar apparatus was discussed in Parliament and by 1816 the Government set up ninety-seven mortar stations with apparatus to be used under the direction of the Water Guard (later HM Coastguard).[2] In a report to the Government, Manby used testimonials from shipwrecked crews to support the use of the apparatus he had designed; two of these related to Sunderland ships and crews.

The first was the master and five crew of the Sunderland brig *Nancy* who wrote of their experience when their ship was stranded off Yarmouth in December 1809. They said that they had to tie themselves to the rigging to avoid being washed overboard by huge waves. They told how Captain Manby had fired a rope with a hooked shot which held securely onto the ship and which enabled a boat to be hauled from the shore to rescue them, 'otherwise we must inevitably have perished.'[3]

The replica Manby Mortar on display in Roker Watch House.

The same rescue was witnessed by Thomas Stoddart, master of the brig *Camilla*, also of Sunderland, whose ship was stranded nearby. He wrote confirming the actions of Manby in rescuing the *Nancy*'s crew and gave a description of how he and his crew were then rescued by the same method.[4] The first recording of the use of Manby's apparatus in the north-east was in January 1830 when two crew members of the sloop *Glatton* were rescued from the Black Midden rocks at the mouth of the Tyne.[5]

Following the writing of this essay Manby was commissioned by Lord Sidmouth, Secretary of State, to survey the east coast of England in relation to the appropriateness of equipment to be provided.[6] The report, dated 1813, is a descriptive account of the coastal towns and villages with suggestions as to the most useful methods of lifesaving and types of apparatus that should be supplied. In his report Manby describes Sunderland as having many dangerous rocks in front of and extending to each side of the pier. He comments favourably on Sunderland lifeboats, describing them as being particularly worthy of notice having the advantage of being sufficiently buoyant to avoid danger even when filled with men and taking on water.

Manby's view of the Sunderland lifeboats refers to those built by the firm of Wake at Monkwearmouth. These were based on the Greathead principle but constructed on plans suggested by John Davison of Bishopwearmouth, who received a medal from the Royal Humane Society for his ideas.[7] The design for the boats was different from any others in the country. They had fifty to sixty airtight buoyancy compartments, apertures to allow seawater to drain out and the seating was arranged down the centre to aid stability. An iron keel added strength and ballast, and there were ropes around the gunwales to help prevent people being washed overboard.[8]

Henry Trengrouse (1772 – 1854), who lived on the south coast, had also witnessed a tragedy when the frigate *Anson* was lost with about 100 lives in December 1807 near Loe Bar, Cornwall. He invented apparatus that was similar to Manby's but used a rocket instead of a mortar and also a chair to transport people. Rockets were quicker and much lighter than mortars, which made his apparatus easier to use and to transport to the site of a wreck. In 1818 Trengrouse exhibited his apparatus to the Admiralty where it was agreed that this was the best means of lifesaving as it was more accurate and easier to use than the mortar apparatus. It was decided that sets be commissioned and sent to dockyards around the country, although it is almost certain that this did not actually take place.[9]

The first record of lifesaving apparatus with rockets being used to attempt to rescue a shipwrecked crew in the north-east of England was in 1842 when the *Cato* went on to rocks at Souter Point, Whitburn near Sunderland. It was reported that the local rector had been prominent in organising a lifesaving company with rocket apparatus which was used efficiently by the men on shore. Unfortunately, the ship's crew did not know how to use the lines and the rescue had to be made by a lifeboat.[10] This example helps to illustrate that, while there were the means of saving lives, and people were willing to promote and finance them, there was no co-ordinated approach across either the region or the country.

There were several other men who worked on developing rockets for use in lifesaving. William Congreve (1772 – 1828) worked on adapting military rockets in 1822 by adding an attachment for a line and a grappling hook. John Dennett(1780 – 1852) trialled a series of shore-to-ship rockets during 1826 and 1827. He won national acclaim in 1832 when nineteen men were rescued from the merchant ship *Bainbridge* using rocket apparatus. By 1853 about 120 coastguard stations were equipped with the Dennett lifesaving equipment and many others used other equipment devised by Manby, Trengrouse and Carte.

The most enduring of the rocket apparatus was that designed by Edward Mourier Boxer (d.1898). His invention was a two-stage rocket which was mounted on a central guide stick. This design made it more effective as extra range could be achieved and the double action caused less strain to the line so it was less likely to part. The Boxer rocket was introduced in 1865 and was still in use after the Second World War.

The Board of Trade supplied all the apparatus to coastguard stations, but even some of the larger stations had only two or three coastguards on duty at a time. Therefore at times of great

Illustration of early
lifesavers with a
Manby Mortar.

The memorial to Henry Trengrouse. (By kind permission of Helston Museum, Cornwall)

need, for example during severe weather, the coastguards were often ineffective due to lack of numbers.[11] It was incidents such as these that led to the setting up of the VLBs across the country to ensure that sufficient numbers of trained men were available to assist with lifesaving.

The use of lifesaving apparatus from the shore remained the province of the HM Coastguard, which was instituted in 1822. It adopted an instruction of its predecessor, the Water Guard, that 'when a wreck takes place on any part of the coast every officer and man on the spot, or stationed within a reasonable distance, is to afford every assistance for the purpose of saving the lives of the persons aboard.'[12] In 1856, the earliest year for which figures are available, the Board of Trade statistics show that 2,231 lives were saved by all methods including lifeboats and shore-based apparatus.[13] The coastguards complemented the use of lifeboats run by the Royal National Lifeboat Institution (RNLI) and private lifesaving companies.

Lifeboats had been available in some parts of the country from the late eighteenth century, mainly through privately funded or charitable schemes; for example, a coble was converted for lifesaving in Bamburgh on the north-east coast in 1786.[14] This was organised by Archdeacon John Sharp of Durham who had realised the need for some organisation for lifesaving in the area. The coble was sent to London to be converted by coachbuilder Lionel Lukin and it was on station at Bamburgh in 1787.[15]

In South Shields two years later the wreck of the brig *Adventure* was the catalyst for a group of shipowners commissioning designs for a boat that 'could be launched into large waves for the purpose of saving life.'[16] The result of this was the commissioning of Henry Greathead to build a vessel to a specific design, which meant that South Shields was the first town in the country to have the services of a purpose-built lifeboat. Within the following eight years the boat and crew saved some 200 lives.[17]

The story was similar in Sunderland where again the shipowners set up a committee to raise money for the first lifeboat. One was built to the Greathead design by William Wake of Bishopwearmouth and was in place in 1800.[18] In 1811 another Sunderland boat was fitted with watertight compartments to improve buoyancy.[19] The first boat placed in Sunderland by the RNLI was the *Florence Nightingale* in April 1865.[20]

Interestingly, this boat was purchased with money raised by the people of Derby in the Midlands. An article in the *Sunderland Herald* reported that the people of Derby, supported by several prominent citizens, decided to raise money for a lifeboat to be presented by the RNLI and to be stationed by them at a place on the coast that was in need. The Institution made the decision that the boat would be placed at Sunderland and a celebration was held in Derby to hand it over. The Sunderland lifeboat crew attended and there was a regatta on the river. The boat was named after Florence Nightingale, who was a native of Derby, and it was transported to Sunderland on 24 April 1865.[21]

There was no co-ordinated approach to lifesaving until steps were taken by Sir William Hillary, now recognised as the founder of the RNLI. In 1823 he made an appeal for the foundation of a lifeboat service which put forward six advantages of an organised service. These were that the preservation of human lives from shipwreck was to be the first consideration, then

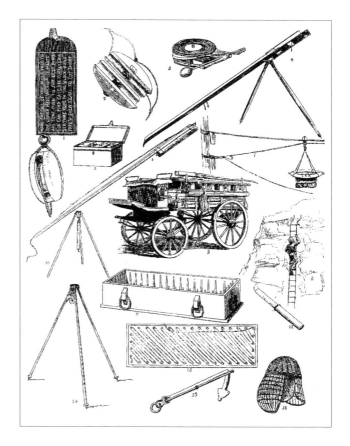

Sketch of the lifesaving apparatus.

The lifeboat at Sunderland South Pier. (By kind permission of Sunderland Antiquarian Society)

The wreck of the *Stanley* at Tynemouth, 1864. (By kind permission of North Tyneside Council)

The watch house of Tynemouth Volunteer Life Brigade.

assistance to vessels in distress and their crews, then the preservation of vessels and property, the prevention of plunder, followed by succour and support for those rescued, and the bestowing of reward to those who made rescues and provision for those widowed or orphaned.[22] Hillary made good use of influential friends and a meeting was called on 4 March 1824 at which the National Institution for the Preservation of Life from Shipwreck was founded.[23] It became responsible for the provision and manning of lifeboats around Great Britain and was later renamed the RNLI.

This latter part of the nineteenth century was the time when there was a growing awareness of safety issues, and the developments in lifesaving and the formation of VLBs can be seen as part of a growing local and national picture to seek means to prevent wrecks and to save lives.

In 1864 the wreck of the *Stanley* at the entrance to the River Tyne marked the next and most important development in lifesaving from shipwrecks. The Tynemouth Volunteer Life Brigade was the first to be set up in the country and it was founded following the wreck of the *Stanley* during severe gales on 24 November 1864.

In the early evening, in the midst of a strong gale with tremendous seas, the steamship *Stanley* was carried onto the notorious Black Midden rocks, holing her bottom and flooding her boiler fires. She was carrying about sixty passengers and crew as well as livestock. Four local lifeboats put to sea but none could reach her due to the high seas. The coastguards rigged up the shore-based rocket apparatus and got a line on board but the crew secured it incorrectly and it could not be used. Eventually a line was properly secured and some of the people were taken off before the line snagged. Large crowds had heard the maroons being sent up to call the lifeboat crews and hundreds of people watched as many attempts were made to save the stricken crew and passengers, but about half of the people on board were drowned. In all, four ships were wrecked at the mouth of the River Tyne that day with the loss of about thirty-four lives.[24]

One of the witnesses, John Morrison, was convinced that local men, trained in the use of lifesaving apparatus, could have assisted the coastguards and helped to prevent loss of life. Morrison discussed this idea with the Quaker brothers, John Foster and Joseph Spence, who decided that this was a venture they wished to support.[25] John Foster Spence wrote to the *Shields Gazette* and in his letter, published on 1 December 1864, he referred to the inquest into the loss of the *Stanley*. He proposed the setting up of a volunteer force that would be trained by the coastguard to assist them. A public meeting was called and held on 5 December 1864 which resulted in over 140 volunteers putting themselves forward for training, and on 9 December the Committee of the Borough of Tynemouth Life Saving Brigade met for the first time.[26]

John Foster Spence, by then the Honorary Secretary, wrote to the Board of Trade in December 1864 forwarding a copy of the proposed rules for the Tynemouth brigade. He referred to the wreck of the *Stanley* and stressed that assistance could have been provided if men had been trained. He also expressed the hope that the setting up of the Tynemouth brigade would see the start of a movement throughout the country.[27] The Board replied in early January 1865, stating their acceptance of the services of a valuable means of assisting the coastguard and suggesting that it be made clear in the rules that the brigade would act under the command of the coastguard.

John Foster Spence

It was the work done mainly by John Foster Spence, assisted by his brother Joseph and others, that has earned him recognition as the founder of the Volunteer Life Brigades. He was born in 1818 in North Shields, the son of a draper and banker, Robert Spence. Being from a Quaker family, he was educated at the Friend's School, York. In 1843 he married Elizabeth Corder at Chelmsford and together they had six children.

He served on the local council in Tynemouth for many years, was elected mayor in 1861 and an alderman in 1862. He retired from the council in 1867 but returned as a councillor three years later, being elected mayor for a second time in 1891. Throughout his adult life he worked hard in the public sphere, being involved in and working on many bodies including the Board of Guardians, the School Board, Indigent Sick Society, Bible Society, Tyne Lifeboat Institution and the Northern Society for the Blind.[28]

His philanthropic and charitable works earned him great renown in the region, and his work in the formation of the Tynemouth VLB was typical of his efforts to improve the lives of ordinary people. His correspondence with the Board of Trade at the time of establishing the brigade, and the setting up of the rules under which it would work, shows how actively he was involved and how hard he worked to promote a cause which became a national institution. He died on 22 July 1901 at the grand age of eighty-two years after a long illness, and was mourned not only by the people of Tynemouth but by all of those associated with the Volunteer Life Brigade movement.

John Foster Spence, the founder of Volunteer Life Brigades. (By kind permission of North Tyneside Council)

The watch house of South Shields Volunteer Life Brigade.

South Shields soon followed the example of the men on the north side of the Tyne with a meeting held in December 1865, in the Mechanics' Institute, to discuss the formation of a brigade. As with Sunderland some years later, the movement was taken forward by a petition being presented to the mayor, Alderman Moffet, and a public meeting was held which led to 147 volunteers being enrolled.[29]

The main effect of the *Stanley* disaster and the actions taken by the people of Tynemouth was that the Board of Trade was so pleased with the setting up of the brigade that they forwarded a copy of its rules to every coastguard station in the country to attempt to get other similar brigades established.[30] The Board drew up the circular, describing it as being a consequence of the success of the Tynemouth VLB and an understanding of the need in other parts of the country, in order to counteract a proposal put forward by central government that the numbers of coastguards be cut.[31]

It proposed two options: in places where the coastguard wished to enrol a few men to assist them, Volunteer Life Saving Companies could be established. These were expected to be small in size and on the more isolated parts of the coast where cover by the coastguard was limited. They were under the direct control of the coastguard; in larger ports and around busy areas of coast where larger numbers of volunteers were needed, Life Brigades could be set up and these would be run, and to a great extent financed, by local committees.

The notes made by Board officials show their concerns that payments to volunteers and brigades could become an expensive undertaking. They clearly saw their role as controlling and directing the actions of the brigades rather than managing them on a day-to-day basis. The Board of Trade set out their proposals outlining the respective responsibilities of the parties involved. The Board would supply all apparatus and rent for accommodation to house it. The coastguard was to be responsible for inspecting the brigades on a regular basis, instructing the volunteers in the use of apparatus and taking charge at rescues. Brigades and their members had

Sketch of apparatus with rocket in launcher.

to undertake drill regularly, wear a distinguishing badge, obey the rules set out by the Board and return annual accounts.[32]

The Board also published instructions in September 1866 to instruct the coastguard and brigades in the use of rocket and mortar apparatus, and advise on how to revive people who were apparently drowning.[33] The actions of central government were, however, fairly limited in terms of enforcing higher standards across the nation, and a great reliance was placed on local initiatives and funding. The reliance for ensuring that central government legislation and guidance was implemented was placed on individuals who were prepared to donate funds, organise men and manage these institutions, and on those who were prepared to volunteer for service.

The use of volunteers in sea rescue does have parallels in other industries. The use of volunteers, for instance, in mine rescues during the nineteenth and very early twentieth centuries, shows just how willing ordinary working men were to put themselves at risk to save the lives of their fellows. It can be said that the qualities of human compassion, bravery and concern for others are common to those people who volunteer for both mining and sea rescues.

Bearing in mind the pace at which the coal mining industry developed, it is perhaps surprising that it was not until after a Royal Commission in 1910 that an organised rescue service for the mining industry became a requirement.[34] Prior to this it was left to volunteers at a colliery where a disaster occurred, possibly along with workers from neighbouring mines, to effect a rescue. Records of pit disasters during the period show that there was never a lack of volunteers who went ahead with rescues, even when the hope of success was minimal and the risk of death or injury in entering a dangerous mine was present.[35]

Although at the time they were not organised as a service in the way in which the VLBs were, this does provide a parallel in terms of volunteers providing a service which, it may be thought, should have been funded and managed by local or central government. The detail in the records of the types of rescues undertaken by the VLBs clearly illustrates that these men were putting their own lives at risk on a regular basis, as well as spending many hours in training and drilling.

Notes

1 W.B.C. Probert, 'The Evolution of Rocket-Based Maritime Rescue Systems in the First Half of the Nineteenth Century', *The Mariner's Mirror*, Vol.83 No.4 November 1997, pp.434-5

2 Ibid, p.436

3 Robinson Library, Special Collections, Grey Tracts, Vol.101, G.W. Manby, 'Essay on the Preservation of Shipwrecked Persons', 1812

4 Ibid.

5 Probert, 'The Evolution of Rocket-Based Maritime Rescue Systems', p.440

6 Robinson Library, Special Collections, Grey Tracts Vol.101, G.W. Manby, General Report on the Survey of the Eastern Coast of England, 1813

7 W. Mitchell, *History of Sunderland,* (Manchester: Morten, reprinted 1972), p.77

8 M.A. Richardson, *The Local Historian's Table Book,* (Newcastle: Richardson, 1842), pp.415-6

9 Probert, 'The Evolution of Rocket-Based Maritime Rescue Systems', pp. 437-41

10 *Newcastle Weekly Chronicle,* 12 October 1904, p.4

11 W. Webb, *Official History of HM Coastguard,* (London: HMSO, 1976), p.66

12 Webb, *Official History of HM Coastguard,* p.56

13 Ibid.

14 A. Beilby, *Heroes All! The Story of the RNLI,* (Yeovil: Patrick Stephens Ltd, 1992), pp.21-22

15 Ibid.

16 A. Gale, *Wrecks and Rescues: Shelter from the Storm,* (Newcastle; Keepdate Ltd, 1993), p.5

17 Ibid, p.6

18 Ibid, p.8

19 Ibid.

20 *Sunderland Daily Echo,* 28 April 1865, p.8

21 Ibid.

22 City of Sunderland Library, 'An appeal to the British Nation on the Humanity and Policy of Forming a National Institution for the Preservation of Lives from Shipwreck', Sir William Hillary, 1823

23 Beilby, *Heroes All!* p.20

24 B. Whittaker, *A Trilogy of Lifesaving,* Vol.1 pp.102-7

25 B. Whittaker, *A Trilogy of Lifesaving,* Vol.3 pp.1-2

26 C.A. de W. Kitcat, 'Volunteer Life Brigades of the North East Coast', *The Coastguard,* Vol.18 No.3 Article 1, p.68

27 National Archive, MT 9/22, Tynemouth VLB Board's Approval of Rules, 1864.

28 North Tyneside Council Local Studies Library, *South Shields Daily News,* 22 July 1901, p.3

29 B. Whittaker, *A Trilogy of Lifesaving,* Vol.2

30 National Archive, MT 9/28, Instructions for Enrolling Volunteer Life Brigades, 1866

31 Ibid.

32 Ibid.

33 Her Majesty's Stationery Office, Board of Trade, 'Instructions in Respect of the Rocket and Mortar Apparatus for Saving Life from Shipwreck and Directions for Restoring the Apparently Drowned', 1866

34 Ibid, p.32

35 Ibid, p.29

two

SUNDERLAND IN THE TIME OF THE DEVELOPMENT OF VOLUNTEER LIFE BRIGADES

The establishment of Volunteer Life Brigades depended, in part, on there being people of wealth and social standing who were willing and able, financially, to support their development, and on there being people with a social conscience to promote their value to commerce and to society. The growth of Sunderland in the nineteenth century as an industrial area meant that a new class of relatively wealthy, and often politically active, people was in a position to devote some of their time and money to promoting and supporting good causes. This solid industrial base allowed organisations such as the Sunderland VLB to be established and developed, but this was also linked to the nature of the industry, politics and society of the town.

The expansion of industry in the Sunderland area was determined by the location of the town at the mouth of the River Wear but also by the geology of the area. The developing industries led to the importation of raw materials and also the export of finished goods. Local raw materials, such as coal and limestone, were exported through the port. Sailing colliers, needing to return to the north in ballast, carried back clay, chalk, sand and flint at little cost to the local industries requiring them.[1]

Limestone was available in exposed positions in the area and was quarried, then taken by wagon-ways to kilns near the riverside to be burnt. It was used as an agricultural fertiliser, in mortar and as a flux in glassmaking, and Sunderland became the main lime-exporting port in the country.[2] Pottery-making was a huge industry in the early nineteenth century, with nearly 300,000 pieces being exported in 1819.[3] Unfortunately the trade declined in the last quarter of the century due to tariff barriers, but at its height huge quantities of white clay were imported from southern England.

In 1877, the year in which Sunderland VLB was founded, there were thirteen glass manufacturers in the town who made a variety of products including bottles, window glass and tableware.[4] There was also a thriving timber trade, mainly from the Baltic, bringing in the timber needed in the shipbuilding, coal mining and engineering industries and for the expanding railway network.[5] Papermaking was an old-established industry in Sunderland, but

Above: Mowbray Park and
the Victoria Hall. (By kind
permission of Sunderland
Antiquarian Society)

Right: The River Wear, *c.*1885. (By
kind permission of Sunderland
Antiquarian Society)

The bridges over the River Wear, 1880. (By kind permission of Sunderland Antiquarian Society)

The Bridge dockyard, 1880. (By kind permission of Sunderland Antiquarian Society)

the development of the use of Esparto grass in the process, first patented in 1865, meant that this began to be imported and subsequently warehousing was provided at the port.[6]

There was a thriving copperas industry based in several places on the river with the largest being at Deptford. This process involved extracting chemicals from pyrites to produce ferrous sulphate and green vitriol; these were used in agriculture, in paper manufacture, and in the production of dyes and inks. Pyrites was brought in through the port from Lyme in Dorset, and this industry continued until 1896. Rope making was already established as an industry on Wearside in the late eighteenth century, using the traditional but very slow method of rope walks.[7]

The need to meet the growing demands of the shipping industry was met by the firm of Webster & Grimshaw who, in 1794 at Deptford in Sunderland, established the world's earliest factory for machine-made rope. In the early nineteenth century new demands from railways and the collieries increased the need for manufacture, which led to increases in imports of hemp and, in the 1830s, the development of wire rope.[8]

The development of Sunderland as a port relied on the shipment of coal, and this in turn was influenced by three main factors: the improvement of the port by the River Wear Commissioners (RWC), the emergence of a network of railways in the area, and the rise in the demand for coal.

The first railways in Sunderland were the wagon-ways that were used to move limestone from quarries to the river. In the early nineteenth century these were developed to bring in coal from County Durham to the port. Until 1879, however, the growth of a borough-wide railway network was hindered by the lack of a bridge over the Wear, and so there were two separate systems on either side of the river. That year saw the building of a major bridge across the Wear to carry the railway, freight and passengers, thereby giving greater access to the docks and harbour.[9]

The demand for coal increased rapidly across the country in the early nineteenth century, mainly due to the development of steam power in industry and also for transportation.[10] The industrial consumption of coal overtook domestic purchasers by 1830, with iron production being the largest consumer. Other industries such as potteries, flourmills, breweries and cotton production also came to rely on coal-based energy.[11]

Shipbuilding in Sunderland was already well established by the late eighteenth century and it became the major industry of the town for many years. The main product of the industry prior to the growth of the mid-nineteenth century was small vessels used for coastal trade. The builders were largely self-employed carpenters and shipwrights, sometimes working together in groups, and they were responsible for the steady growth of the industry. The large family firms that were to dominate the industry worldwide and the economic life of the town began to be established in the early years of the nineteenth century.

The Laing family set up business at Monkwearmouth in 1793 but in 1808 moved to Deptford, the yard from which Sir James Laing later became the most influential of Sunderland's shipbuilders. Luke Crown's yard was established in 1807 and built ships continuously for seventy years. At Monkwearmouth, Peter Austin set up a yard in 1826 and his son Samuel, one of the men involved in setting up the VLB, moved the yard to the south side of the river in 1846. The Bartram and Pickersgill yards were both started in 1838 and Doxford's in 1840, the latter firm later opening at Pallion, which was to become the biggest yard in the town. The Thompson family had yards at North Sands and Southwick and Short's built at Pallion from 1850.

All of these became well-respected and well-known firms within the international shipbuilding industry in the decades up to the start of the First World War.[12] The development on the Wear led to Sunderland being described in the annals of Lloyd's register in 1834 as being 'the most important shipbuilding centre in the country, nearly equalling, as regards number and tonnage of ships built, all the other ports together.'[13] By 1840 there were sixty-five shipyards in Sunderland employing 1,600 shipwrights and producing that year 251 ships at an average of 250 tons.[14] The largest tonnage ever produced by wood shipbuilders was 153 ships with a total of 68,992 tons in 1853.[15]

Two major developments influenced the industry during the nineteenth century: the development of railways to transport goods and passengers, which reduced the demand for small coastal vessels, and the development of steam and ships built of iron and, later, steel. The need for yards to be able to adapt to the technological changes meant that many small firms went out of business, while the larger firms who could invest in changes went on to become the main suppliers.

Steam tugboats had been built on the Wear from 1825 and the first seagoing steamship the *Experiment* was launched in 1845,[16] but the main development came after 1853 with Laing's launching of three steamships in 1855.[17] Steam and sail continued to be built alongside each other, with sail declining until the last ship was built in 1893 by the Pickersgill's yard.[18]

At the same time the transition to building with iron was taking place. The first iron ship launched on the Wear was the *Loftus*, a coaster built by George Clark in 1852. The much larger *Amity* (479 tons) was launched by Laing's in 1853.[19] Very few wooden ships were built after 1863, although many composite ones were produced and the last wooden ship was built in 1880 at the Pickersgill's yard.[20]

As ships got larger and technology progressed many of the smaller yards could not compete, with those left growing larger, developing the use of steel and sophisticated engineering techniques. These developments also meant the dawn of new trades such as boiler making and riveting, as well as a range of ancillary industries, the chief one being marine engineering. By the beginning of the twentieth century, Sunderland had thirteen surviving shipyards launching between sixty and ninety ships a year with a total tonnage of between 200–300,000.[21]

Although coal was a very important factor in the development of the port of Sunderland, there was only one colliery within the borough – at Monkwearmouth. The sinking of Wearmouth colliery was begun in 1826 but it took nine years to complete as the shaft had to be driven through layers of magnesium limestone, and also because of problems with water seepage.[22] It was not until 1835 that the first cargo of coal from the pit was shipped from its own staithes on the riverside. At this date Wearmouth was the deepest coal mine in the world.[23] The importance of the industry, in terms of goods passing through the port and of the population, is reflected in the figures for 1857, by which time the colliery was producing half a million tons of coal a year and employing over 1,200 men and boys.[24]

The development of industry in Sunderland around this time, and the context which enabled the setting up of the Sunderland VLB with its promoters among the industrialists and politicians of the day, is best summarised in a quote from the *Daily Telegraph* in 1882. It describes

Overview of Doxford's Shipyard, 1903. (By kind permission of Sunderland Antiquarian Society)

The coal staithes of Wearmouth Colliery, 1908. (By kind permission of Sunderland Antiquarian Society)

Ettrick Quay. (By kind permission of Sunderland Antiquarian Society)

Mowbray Park and the Winter Gardens, 1900. (By kind permission of Sunderland Antiquarian Society)

The new Roker Pier, opened in 1903. (By kind permission of Sunderland Antiquarian Society)

'the wonderful picture of thriving industry which the banks of the Wear presented…every acre of land is the basis of some great commercial undertaking.'[25]

Sunderland became a municipal borough in 1835 with the linking of Bishopwearmouth and Sunderland parishes, and the first town council was established.[26] In 1867 the Sunderland Extension and Improvement Act brought the districts of Hendon, Pallion and Monkwearmouth into the borough.[27] The radicals were becoming stronger at local level with the election of a new group of councillors that included Samuel Storey and Samuel Sinclair Robson.

The election of Storey was an indicator of changes in the make-up of the council during the 1870s. Between 1874 and 1877 the councillors who were elected to fill vacancies were nearly all friends or associates of Storey, or people that he knew through business interests. In October

1878 there were three major political groups in the borough: Storey's radicals numbered twenty-eight councillors; there were nineteen Tories and a group of seventeen independent councillors. Many of these men were involved directly, or indirectly through donations, in the setting up of Sunderland VLB.

Sunderland harbour improvements started in 1717 when the RWC were established. Piers to the north and south of the river were replaced or built in the late eighteenth century, but the development of Sunderland's port and harbour took place over many years. A key objective in the nineteenth century was the building of huge breakwaters on either side of the river mouth. Work started on the 2,800ft long new north pier at Roker in 1885 and it was officially opened in 1903. The new south pier was started in 1893 and went on until 1912 when it was concluded with the addition of a round-head.[28]

The nineteenth century was also a time for the development of education and leisure, particularly in terms of the founding of libraries, educational institutions and societies. A subscription library was set up in Sunderland in 1795 in High Street, founded by a group of leading citizens.[29] It became so popular that it moved to a new purpose-built building in Fawcett Street in 1878 to give better facilities to its 1,000 members.[30] From 1858 there was also a free public library in the Athenaeum building in Fawcett Street where books were available.

The Sunderland Museum was also in the Athenaeum and was very popular, with the attendance figures for 1855 showing that 10,000 visitors went to see the collections of shells, minerals and curiosities.[31] By the late 1870s the popularity of such attractions led to Sunderland Corporation funding the building of a new museum and library to house the town's collections, which was opened in 1879[32] and is still in use as a museum and art gallery.

Sunderland had a Mechanics' Institute which was one of the first set up in the country, along with Alnwick and Newcastle. These were founded within one year of the first institute being established in London in 1823.[33] Public parks were also provided by the Corporation to provide fresh air and open spaces as the town grew larger, with Mowbray Park in the town centre being opened in 1857 and extended a few years later.[34]

Sunderland was, therefore, not only subject to industrial growth but also to the influences of education, philanthropy and a drive by local government and individuals to improve the lives of its population. This selective view of the town in the nineteenth century does show a place of contrasts: a heavily industrialised town but also one in which social care was being developed and philanthropic organisations were being set up to promote the well-being of working-class people. There were men of wealth and social standing who used their involvement in institutions, such as the SVLB, to promote their business and personal interests. Alongside this there was a skilled working class with more time to address issues such as education and leisure and, through these, to wider urbanising influences.[35] The key factors were in place in Sunderland in the mid-eighteenth century for institutions such as the SVLB to be established, manned and maintained.

Notes

1　N.T. Sinclair, 'Industry to 1914' in G.E. Milburn & S.T. Miller (eds) *Sunderland River, Town and People* (Sunderland: Sunderland Borough Council, 1990), p.23

2　Ibid, p.21

3　Ibid, p.24

4　Ibid, pp.25, 32

5　Ibid, p.28

6　G.L. Dodds, *A History of Sunderland* (Sunderland: Albion Press, 2nd edn, 2001), p.112

7　Rain's *Eye Plan of Sunderland*, drawn between 1785-1790, shows several examples of rope walks

8　Sinclair, 'Industry to 1914', pp.29-30

9　Ibid, pp.26-7

10　R. Church, *The History of the British Coal Industry*, Vol.3 Victorian Pre-eminence (Oxford: Clarendon Press, 1986), p.4

11　Ibid, p.5

12　J.F. Clarke, 'Shipbuilding 1780-1914', in G.E. Milburn & S.T. Miller (eds) *Sunderland River, Town and People* (Sunderland: Sunderland Borough Council, 1990), pp.33-6

13　Smith & Holden, *Where Ships are Born*, p.1

14　Corfe, *History of Sunderland*, p.76

15　Smith & Holden, *Where Ships are Born*, p.2

16　Corfe, History of Sunderland, p.77

17　Ibid.

18　Corfe, *History of Sunderland*, p.77

19　J. Clarke, 'Shipbuilding 1780-1914', in G.E. Milburn & S.T. Miller (eds) *Sunderland River, Town and People* (Sunderland: Sunderland Borough Council, 1990), p.37

20　Corfe, *History of Sunderland*, p.77

21　Corfe, *History of Sunderland*, p.78

22　Sinclair, 'Industry to 1914', p.24

23　Ibid.

24　Corfe, *History of Sunderland*, p.84

25　Ibid, p.78

26　Dodds, *A History of Sunderland*, p.89

27　P.J. Storey, *Personalities and Power*, p.123

28　S.T. Miller, 'Harbour and River Improvement' in G.E. Milburn & S.T. Miller (eds) *Sunderland River, Town and People* (Sunderland: Sunderland Borough Council, 1990), p.19

29　G.E. Milburn, 'Education and Learning 1780-1914' in G.E. Milburn & S.T. Miller (eds) *Sunderland River, Town and People* (Sunderland: Sunderland Borough Council, 1990), p.148

30　J. Kitts, 'The Sunderland Subscription Library', Antiquities of Sunderland, Vol.9 1908.

31　Dodds, *A History of Sunderland*, p.100.

32　Ibid.

33　'Mechanics' Institutes in North East England', *Durham County Local History Society*, Bulletin 54 (May 1995), pp.34-51

34　Dodds, *A History of Sunderland*, p.100

35　R.J. Morris, 'Clubs, societies and associations', in F.M.L. Thompson (ed.) *The Cambridge Social History of Britain 1750-1950*, Vol.3: Social Agencies and Institutions (Cambridge: Cambridge University Press, 1990), p.418

three

THE ESTABLISHMENT OF SUNDERLAND VOLUNTEER LIFE BRIGADE

The First Sunderland Volunteer Life Brigade

The organisation that is now known as the Sunderland Volunteer Life Brigade was established in 1877. This date, however, poses the question as to the reasons for the brigade in Sunderland being set up more than ten years later than the first brigades in Tynemouth and South Shields. It seems unusual that a busy port such as Sunderland would not have set up a brigade years earlier, especially with the proximity of those on the Tyne and the publicity that these would have prompted.

Research has shown that an earlier brigade was originally set up in Sunderland in 1866, the same year as the South Shields brigade. It was formed by the RWC at a meeting held on 3 July 1866, at which a letter was read from the Surveyor General of the Board of Trade suggesting the formation of a VLB.[1] This was one of a number of such letters that were sent to coastal towns and ports after the establishment of the Tynemouth VLB to encourage the setting up of brigades around the country.[2]

The RWC dock master was given the task of forming a brigade from the men employed by the RWC on the understanding that they would be allowed to train during work time.[3] This brigade was to be called the South Dock (Sunderland) Volunteer Life Brigade and seventy-two of the RWC's employees enrolled. Rules for the conduct of the brigade were drawn up and sent to the Board of Trade for approval; these were accepted and the Board subscribed 10 guineas to the brigade's funds.[4] The RWC also made over a building as a meeting and training place for the brigade volunteers.

Very little further information can be found about the activities or running of this first VLB in Sunderland. It was still in existence in 1870 when an incident occurred following a rescue from the schooner *Vision* – there was an altercation between a member of HM Coastguard and the rescuers, the VLB and the lifeboat crew, as detailed in Neil Mearn's history of the River

Wear Watch.[5] After this no further record has been found to date. It is possible that this first brigade remained very much the province of the RWC and its employees, rather than being viewed as a resource of the town as a whole.

It does also seem that various attempts were made to re-establish a VLB in Sunderland before 1877. In November 1875 the *Sunderland Daily Echo* reported that Captain William Coulson (later a founder member of the brigade) had suggested this and proposed that three divisions be set up – one for the north pier, one for the south pier and the third to cover the south outlet and Hendon.[6] It was, however, to be another two years before a brigade was re-established.

Foundation of the Current Sunderland Volunteer Life Brigade

The beginning of the current Sunderland VLB was a talk given on 20 February 1877 by Mr Henry C. Spence, a relative of John Foster Spence, one of the founders of the Tynemouth brigade. Henry addressed a meeting of the Salem Chapel Young Men's Improvement Society in Sunderland on the subject of life brigades, using the Tynemouth brigade as an example of the work, and he raised the issue of a need for a similar brigade in Sunderland.[7] The talk was reported in the local press and, by 8 March 1877, a petition signed by some 130 people was presented to the mayor requesting that a public meeting be held to consider forming a VLB in Sunderland.[8]

Samuel Storey was the Mayor of Sunderland at this time. He had entered local politics in 1865 being elected as a councillor for Monkwearmouth in 1869. In 1873, along with other liberal activists, he founded the *Sunderland Daily Echo*, of which he later became managing proprietor.[9] Storey probably put forward an article to the *Sunderland Daily Echo* promoting the formation of the Sunderland VLB.[10]

The public meeting, held on 19 March 1877, was attended by over 300 people. Captain Johnson, chief of the coastguard district between Blyth and Saltburn, proposed the formation of a brigade in Sunderland to 'assist in the saving of life in cases of shipwreck occurring on the coast.'[11] The speed at which these meetings were set up, and the public support given, showed that a need had been recognised.

The discussion and decisions at the meetings also give an idea of the format that was expected. Various conditions were set out, in line with other brigades, to which all volunteers had to agree to before being accepted. These included being under the command of the senior office of the coastguard, implicit obedience to the senior officer present and, if required, enrolment as special constables. The members would also be expected to help prevent plunder at a shipwreck and assist in delivering property to the Receiver of Wrecks.

The Organisation of the Brigade and Election of Captains

By early July 1877, 122 volunteers had been enrolled and the brigade was in a position to start to organise them. A committee was set up to manage the brigade and to elect officers to run the practical side. It also had to be organised so that both the north and

Samuel Storey, Mayor of Sunderland who promoted the founding of Sunderland Volunteer Life Brigade. (By kind permission of *Sunderland Echo*)

William Crute, the First Captain of No. 5 company.

Anthony Brown, the First Captain of No. 4 company.

John Stephenson, Deputy Captain 1877.

south of the river mouth were adequately covered. It was decided that the brigade would comprise five companies, with three based south of the River Wear and two in the north at Monkwearmouth. The divisions became known as the Sunderland South division and the Roker division.

Each company was to have a captain and a deputy captain who would be decided by a ballot of the members. The committee were keen to get the training underway and so held the election for officers on 9 July. The captains for the three southern divisions were William Coulson, who became the senior captain, Hartley Kayll and John Gaine, and for the two northern divisions Anthony Brown and William Crute.

Each company was to have twenty-five members and the brigadesmen were able to choose under whom they would serve, but this was also dependent on where they lived. Call outs for the brigadesmen would be by signal guns, so it was necessary for men to live near the watch house where they were based so that they would hear the signal and be able to respond promptly.

The Record of Drills of the Roker Division for 1895 shows how local the men were to that area. All but four of the men lived in the Roker and Monkwearmouth districts of Sunderland, that is within approximately one mile of the north-side watch house. This was similar to other brigades; in the period 1897 – 8 at Tynemouth VLB only four members lived more than one and a half miles from their watch house.[12]

The First Officers of Sunderland VLB	
Division and Company	**Name**
Sunderland South No.1 Company	Capt. William Coulson
	Dep. Capt. John W. Broderick
Sunderland South No.2 Company	Capt. Hartley Kayll
	Dep. Capt. John J. Kayll
Sunderland South No.3 Company	Capt. John Gaine
	Dep. Capt. Henry C Spence
Roker No.4 Company	Capt. Anthony Brown
	Dep. Capt. John Stephenson
Roker No.5 Company	Capt. William Crute
	Dep. Capt. William Milburn

Another important aspect of setting up was the provision and placing of watch houses at each side of the mouth of the river. The watch houses would be used as bases for the two divisions where some training would take place and equipment could be stored. They also provided a place from which the brigadesmen would keep watch on the coastline and harbour, especially in times of bad weather, for any ships in danger.

John Herring's sketch of the first Sunderland Volunteer Life Brigade drill. (By kind permission of Anne Williams and John Dale)

By July 1878, when the first annual meeting was held, sites had been agreed for watch houses. One for the Sunderland division near the south pier was to be built with funding from the Board of Trade. The RWC granted possession of an existing building on the north pier for the Roker division and, along with the War Office, arranged for the acquisition and placement of signal guns.

The role of the VLB was to provide assistance to the coastguards in the event of a shipwreck within their area. So the key initial element was to train the volunteers in the use of the rocket apparatus so that the brigade would be prepared to assist a ship in distress. The coastguards were experienced in using the apparatus and were responsible for training the VLB members.

They held the first drill in Sunderland at the north pier the day after the election of the captains. Captain Johnson of the coastguard and his men explained the use of the equipment and Captain Coulson of the VLB was then allowed to fire the rocket carrying the line. A demonstration was then given of the use of the apparatus with Captain Coulson being carried between the piers in the breeches buoy and the lines being worked by the coastguards. At the end of the drill Captain Johnson expressed his pleasure at the progress made and said that he would be sending a favourable report to the Board of Trade as the Sunderland brigade had been quicker at this first drill than others who had been practising for months.[13]

Captain William Coulson

The first senior captain of the brigade was William Coulson and he was a driving force in its formation, having campaigned for a brigade in Sunderland for some years. Coulson was a local man born in Sunderland in 1820, the son of a ship's captain. He served his apprenticeship as a carpenter and on completion went to sea where, within three years, he had worked his way from being ship's carpenter to captain. He worked for sixteen years in the trade with China and became very well known and respected in maritime circles.

Coulson went into partnership with a shipowner of South Shields, Mr Kelso, and the wealth he then acquired allowed him to retire from the sea in his mid-forties. He was returned as Conservative councillor for the east end of Sunderland in around 1872 and was, for many years, an overseer of Sunderland parish and a member of Sunderland Board of Guardians.

In May 1877, while the Sunderland VLB was being formed, William Coulson played a key part in a rescue from the *Julia Ravenna*, an Italian barque. All but three of the crew had been taken off this stricken vessel which struck rocks after a tug line parted. As it became clear that the vessel was breaking up and the captain would not leave, Coulson took off his overcoat and was hauled over to the ship in a breeches buoy across very high seas. After much persuasion the captain, chief engineer and a third man agreed to leave the ship via the breeches buoy. Within a couple of hours the ship had been totally wrecked.

Elected as the first senior captain of the SVLB in 1877, Coulson served only a few months before he died at the early age of fifty-seven years on 7 April 1878. A few weeks before his death, he had commanded the brigade at a drill held in the presence of the Earl of Durham, one of the sponsors of the Brigade.[14] The report of his funeral on 10 April showed the great respect in which he was held by the people of Sunderland, with the police band heading the funeral procession from his home in Mowbray Terrace to Sunderland cemetery. Sixty members of the VLB in full uniform accompanied their captain on his final journey.[15]

The strength of the brigade by the end of its first year was 137 volunteers, and four stations had been set up where lifesaving apparatus was stored and where drills could be held. These were at the north pier, south pier, south entrance and Ryhope sands. Drills were held at least every four weeks with the numbers attending ranging between fifty-five and seventy men.[16]

The high profile that was given to organisations such as the brigade was highlighted when the Sunderland VLB was chosen to be part of a short visit by Prince Alfred Ernest, Duke of Edinburgh and the son of Queen Victoria, to Sunderland in 1880. He inspected the brigade house and the men, and also watched a successful demonstration drill with the apparatus.[17]

Financing the Work of the Brigade

The Sunderland VLB was, and continues to be, run almost entirely on voluntary contributions, so fundraising was an important subject for the committee. Donations and subscriptions totalling £180-6-0 were received during the first year of operation, coming from a variety of sources but mainly from local businesses and businessmen. The local nobility, the Marquis of

Early picture of Sunderland Volunteer Life Brigade, date unknown.

John Herring's sketch of the visit of the Duke of Edinburgh, 1880. (By kind permission of Anne Williams and John Dale)

Londonderry and the Earl of Durham contributed 5 guineas each and these two continued to support the brigade by giving donations and attending drills for many years.

Among the subscribers and donors were the local shipbuilders James Laing, William Doxford and Samuel Austin and six individuals or firms of ships brokers. Francis Corder, who later became one of the captains of the brigade, was a partner in the wholesale grocery firm of Pearman & Corder. Both partners were subscribers and their firm was probably a supplier to many of the ships who sailed from the port.

Other local businesses involved were coal fitters, an insurance agent, a miller and a solicitor. One subscriber at least benefited from their connection with the brigade. The drapery firm of Jopling & Tuer gave £1-0-0 to the funds, but an examination of the accounts for that first year shows that they gained over £70 of business as they supplied over 100 guernseys, known locally as 'ganseys', thick sweaters embroidered with the initials of the brigade: SVLB for the southern division and RVLB for the northern one. Indeed most of the expenditure of the first year was on equipment and uniforms; 100 sou'westers were purchased for use by the brigadesmen, as well as caps and ribbons. The caps had the initials of the brigades in gold letters with the officers' caps also having a crown.

Printing and stationery took up a portion of the income as rules had to be printed and articles placed in the press. It is interesting to note that, even though the coastguard was technically in command of the brigade, they were paid for attendance at drills whilst the brigadesmen were not.

At the end of the first year the brigade, despite the initial costs of setting up, were left with a balance of over £50. Cash donations and subscriptions formed the major part of the brigade's income but there were also numerous donations in kind from local businesses, particularly when there was notice in the press that items were needed. The building and equipping of the Roker and Sunderland watch houses brought a very wide range of materials and furnishings as donations.

The accounts for 1878 – 9 show that over £22 worth of goods were received, including gas pipes and fittings and glass for windows, as well as everyday items such as crockery, books and pictures to make the watch houses more comfortable for the men on watch, and for the comfort of shipwrecked crews who may be accommodated.[18] The value of the items donated and the names of the donors were reported in the published annual reports, which would ensure that gifts were noted by the wider community. It also should be remembered, however, that some members of the committee were influential businessmen and there may have been an advantage to them becoming involved in this way.

The donors for the same period were a mixture of larger businesses, including James Hartley's Wear Glass Works, and small local firms such as Ridgeway's Ironmongers and Hill's booksellers. During 1879-80 goods to the value of almost £70 were donated to build and equip the new watch house for the Roker division including windows, chimneys and coals.

In comparison to some other brigades, Sunderland was well funded and supported by businesses and prominent people within the town. The Cullercoats VLB, founded in 1865, was in a poor financial state in August 1887. It was a large brigade, similar in size to Sunderland having over 140 members, but its income in the period was only five shillings and ten pence.[19] The Sunderland brigade in the same period received over £40 in cash as well as numerous donations of goods to equip the watch houses and provide for the men whilst on duty.

Captain Francis Corder.

The reasons for the low income at Cullercoats are not recorded, although as a relatively small fishing village it would not have had the number of wealthy businessmen to provide funding. In addition, the brigade members were nearly all fishermen,[20] possibly spending periods of time away from home and therefore unable to fundraise effectively. An enquiry recommended that the Cullercoats brigade be reduced in number to 100 men, as this would lower costs without compromising efficiency.

The Cullercoats brigade had a much more successful year in financial terms between 1887-8. This may have been because members felt compelled to raise funds because of the debt. Another factor was that the brigade undertook a rescue in March 1888 and assisted in saving the lives of thirteen crew members of the *Czar*. This action would have raised interest in the brigade's work and in providing financial support. The statement of funds shows that over £30 was raised from sources such as church collections and concerts.[21]

The comparison between the Sunderland and Cullercoats brigades, and the information from the Board of Trade records, raises several points of interest about the funding and management of VLBs. The most important one is that the financial management, and therefore to an extent the efficiency, of brigades was very much at a local level. The Board of Trade did provide annual grants depending on size and efficiency of a brigade but these were relatively small amounts. Sunderland's grant of £25 would be one of the highest, bearing in mind its size and the recognition that it was one of the most efficient.

It is also apparent that each brigade committee decided the way in which the grant was spent; some, like Cullercoats and Whitehaven, used the grant to pay their members, whilst the brigadesmen at Sunderland and Tynemouth did not receive any payment for attending drills or rescues. Any additional funds needed for equipment, maintaining watch houses or training had to be raised locally and, therefore, it was important for brigades to keep a high profile to ensure that they were seen as a 'good cause' among the local people who had the desire and the money to provide support.

Sketch of Sunderland brigadesman in original uniform.

Sketch of Sunderland brigadesman in wet weather gear.

9

Donations in Articles, Material, and Labovr towards the Erection and Furnishing of Watch House North Pier.

	£	s	d
Mr. James Armitage, Bay Window & Sashes ...	6	6	0
Messrs. Wm. Grimshaw & Son, 1 Ton of Cement	2	5	0
Sir Hedworth Williamson, Bart., Lime	1	10	0
Messrs. Samuel Tyzack, & Co., 2000 Bricks ...	2	10	0
Mr. John B. Wilkinson, Lead for Bay Window ...	1	10	0
Messrs. Michael Robson & Son, Spouting ...	1	1	0
Messrs. John Blumer, & Co. Wood for Seats ...	0	15	0
Messrs Geo. Swan, & Co., Mantel Piece ...	0	15	0
Mr. John G. Walker, Brass Rod for Mantel Piece ...	0	15	0
Messrs. Kyall, Glass for Windows	0	15	0
Mr George Kirkup, Plate Glass for Look Out ...	0	15	0
Mr. William Smith, Door Frame	0	10	0
Mr. John Thompson, Door	0	5	0
Mr. Thomas Armstrong, Chimney Pot ...	0	2	6
Mr. John Young, Capping	0	2	6
Mr John G. Kirtley, Gas Pipes and Books ...	0	12	6
Mr. William Sanderson, Paint	0	6	0
Robert Thompson, Esq., 50 Vols. Books ...	5	5	0
Mr. Anthony Brown, Tea and Coffee Urns ...	1	10	0
Mr. J. W. Plumb, Binocular Glass	2	10	0
Mr. Hodgson Bell, Clock	0	15	0
Messrs. John Muir & A. Brown, Flag, S.V.L.B.	1	0	0
Mr. R. Alderson, Ensign	0	15	0
Mr. Thomas Wilburn, Books & Brushes ...	0	15	0
Mr. Thomas Dixon, Life Buoy	0	10	0
Messrs. Spain Brothers, Blocks, Rocket Gear for Initiatory Drill	0	10	0
Mr. John Muir, Rope for Initatory Drill ...	0	10	0
Mr. Anthony Scott, Jun., Mugs	0	7	0
Mr. Robert T. Barlow, Oil Painting	3	15	0
Mr. William Greenwell, 1 doz. Spoons	0	5	0
Mr. J. Taylor, Brushes	0	5	0
Mr. John Barlow, Book Case	1	10	0
Mr. Wm. Hill, Unbound Literature	1	0	0
Mr. R. W. Herbert, 1 Ton of Coals	0	10	6
Mr. Chas. T. Thubron, do.	0	10	6
Mr. William Milburn, Book Case	0	12	6
Thomas Elliott, Esq., Spar for Mast ...	0	15	0
William Harty, Esq., Bible	0	10	0
Value of Labour in Mason's, Joiner's, Plumber's, and Painter's Work, contributed by various Members of the Monkwearmouth Division of the Brigade	25	0	0
	£69	**16**	**6**

Donations of goods for the building and furnishing of Roker Watch House, 1880.

The Whitehaven VLB, on the north-west coast of England, was established in 1867.[22] This was a small brigade in comparison with Sunderland and this probably reflects the differences in size and traffic between the two ports. The annual report and accounts of 1869 for the Whitehaven brigade show that, like Sunderland, nearly all the income came from subscriptions and donations, although they also received funding from the Board of Trade. Similarly to Sunderland some local gentry were involved, with the Earl of Lonsdale not only subscribing to the funds but also entertaining the members to supper. Payments to brigadesmen formed the bulk of the expenditure during 1869, being more than half the total income for the year.[23]

The role of lifesaving, the techniques used and the apparatus available were not only a local and national consideration. As early as 1886 the Sunderland VLBs received information on lifesaving in the United States of America in the form of an annual report from the USA. Lifesaving Department. The brigades received donations of these reports until 1901. As well as giving statistical information on the number of rescues undertaken, the reports show some similarities in lifesaving between the two countries. The apparatus used was very similar and there was the joint approach of having lifeboats as well as shore-based apparatus.[24] These reports began to be sent to Sunderland after a visit and attendance at a drill by Lieutenant McLellan of the United States Navy. This drill was put on following a special request from the Board of Trade to demonstrate to Lieutenant McLellan the use of the lifesaving apparatus in Great Britain. The reason for choosing the Sunderland brigades for this demonstration is not stated in the records, but as the annual meeting reports of previous years do comment on the efficiency and skill of the Sunderland brigadesmen it is likely that this brigade was seen as a good example of the work being done nationally by VLBs.

Notes

1 TWAS 202/1053, Minutes of RWC Traffic Committee, 3 July 1866

2 National Archive, MT 9/28 Instructions for enrolling VLBs, 1866

3 TWAS 202/1053 Minutes of RWC Traffic Committee, 14 August 1866

4 TWAS 202/1053 Minutes of RWC Traffic Committee, 28 August 1866.

5 N.W. Mearns, *Sentinels of the Wear: The River Wear Watch*, 1998 p.56

6 *Sunderland Daily Echo*, 17 November 1875

7 *Sunderland Daily Echo*, 21 February 1877, p.3

8 *Sunderland Daily Echo*, 8 March 1877, p.2

9 P.J. Storey, 'Samuel Storey of Sunderland (1841-1925). His Life and Career as a Local Politician and Newspaper Proprietor up to 1895', unpublished thesis M.Litt., University of Edinburgh, 1978

10 *Sunderland Daily Echo*, 24 February 1877, p.2

11 Ibid.

12 Tynemouth VLB

13 *Sunderland Daily Echo*, 11 July 1877, p.2

14 *Sunderland Daily Echo*, 8 April 1878, p.3

15 *Sunderland Daily Echo*, 10 April 1878, p.3

16 Ibid.

17 *Sunderland Daily Echo*, 17 November 1880, p.4

18 *Sunderland Daily Echo*, 19 February 1881, p.2

19 National Archive, MT 9/380, Cullercoats VLB Reports and Contributions, 1878-90

20 Ibid.

21 Ibid.

22 Cumbria Record Office, D Lons/L1/3/545, Minutes of Annual Meeting Whitehaven VLB, 1869

23 Ibid.

24 SVLB, Annual Report of the Operations of the Life Saving Service for the United States, year ending 30 June 1889

four

THE RESCUES 1877–1900

During the mid-nineteenth century, Great Britain had the largest merchant fleet in the world, and the coastal and Baltic trades from the north-east ports formed a large part of the traffic around the British coast. By 1875 almost half of the 2,900 coastal shipwrecks were on the east-coast coal route involving the loss of forty-five lives.[1]

It was within this context that the Volunteer Life Brigade movement was set up. The brigade at Sunderland initially covered an area bounded by Whitburn Steel to the north and Ryhope to the south – approximately six miles of busy coastline. During the winter months, and at times of bad weather on the coast, the two divisions of the brigade were called to keep watch for vessels in need of assistance.

The First Rescue – *Loch Cree*

The first recorded rescue by the Sunderland brigades took place on 14 October 1877, just a few months after its formation, when an iron barque, the *Loch Cree*, became a casualty of a gale and high seas when being towed in to Sunderland harbour. A few minutes before 10.00 p.m. the coastguards fired a rocket to summon the newly formed VLB. The training drills that had been undertaken proved effective as a line was speedily fired to the vessel to take off the crew, but they decided not to leave the ship and the brigadesmen and coastguards stayed on watch in case further help was needed. By 3.00 a.m. the gale had reached an alarming height and the crew signalled for assistance. The brigadesmen fired another rocket which was made fast by the crew and, using the breeches buoy equipment, the eighteen crew members and a pilot were taken off and landed safely within an hour.[2]

The brigade was called out twice in 1878, the first occasion being when the SS *Dorcas* got into difficulties but, although a line was got to the ship, the crew decided to remain on board. Later the brigadesmen attended the schooner *Marcanne*, but she was too far off shore for the apparatus to reach, and the crew were eventually rescued by the lifeboat. Another relatively quiet year in terms of rescues was 1879 with just two call outs. The first was to the schooner *Little Henry* whose crew eventually landed in their own boat and, secondly, to the SS *Viking*, where the crew again decided to remain aboard.

View of Sunderland harbour, date unknown. (By kind permission of Sunderland Antiquarian Society)

Although it may seem that there was little work for the brigadesmen during these times, it must be remembered that they did regular drills with the rocket equipment and also stood on watch over the harbour for any signs of a ship in distress. Without the benefit of modern means of communication, this was the only way to ensure that crews needing assistance would be spotted and a rescue put in place. Many crews, and particularly masters, decided to remain with their ships until disaster was imminent rather than risk losing the ship and its cargo.

October 1880: the *Amelia, Huntly* and *British Ensign*

Severe gales in October 1880 made this the busiest time so far for the VLB, with six attendances from the 27th to the 29th of that month. No rescue had to be effected during the first call out to the ketch *Star* on 21 October, but the next few days brought ferocious gales to the north-east coast which the most experienced sailors said they had not seen for many years. Even the ferries between the two banks of the River Wear had to stop running due to the roughness of the water.

The brigade kept watch at both sides of the harbour from the early evening on 27 October and witnessed three sailing vessels and two steamships reach the safety of the port. Shortly afterwards, a vessel was seen in difficulties near the south entrance. The brigade was signalled and fourteen men of the Southside division, along with Captains Broderick and Wallace, responded as well as six members of the coastguard. The brigantine *Amelia*, which had a Sunderland owner and which was carrying about 40 tons of flint, was grounded on rocks near

Hendon. She had lost most of her masts and the waves were breaking right over her. Within twenty minutes her crew of five had been rescued by the brigade using the rocket apparatus – including Captain Dawson and his son who was the mate.

A survivor, Henry Broomfield, wrote a letter to the *Sunderland Daily Echo* in March 1927, at the time of the brigade's 50th anniversary. He described the wreck, saying how relieved the crew were to see the brigade mustering with the rocket apparatus on shore.[3] During the night the ship was completely wrecked and by morning all that could be seen was her keel with some broken spars attached and timber washed up onto the beach.[4] The sight of the storm and the wreck drew a large crowd of onlookers as the huge waves continued to break right over the harbour.

Captain John W. Broderick

John Watkins Broderick was one of the first officers of Sunderland VLB. He was born in Sunderland in 1831 into a family of seafarers. He was apprenticed to a shipowner and insurance broker being with the firm of G.R. Booth until 1855. He was then employed as a clerk by the Board of Trade in the local marine office. Within twenty years he had risen to the rank of chief superintendent.

He held several appointments in the Grange congregational church where he was a member for forty-six years, and he was also a trustee for the Young Men's Christian Association. His work, in conjunction with William Coulson, in setting up the Sunderland VLB was one of his many philanthropic acts. He was elected as a captain following the death of Captain Coulson in 1878[5] and served with the brigade for many years. He was honorary secretary for the brigade until his death in 1905.[6]

On 28 October 1880 there were four call outs, the first at noon to the brigantine *Huntly* which was wrecked off Ryhope, and her six crew members rescued. The brigade then had to go directly to attend the schooner *Zosteria* which beached, also at Ryhope, but her crew were able to land unassisted. The third call out within three hours followed with the schooner *British Ensign* of Faversham getting into difficulties, again off Ryhope. The vessel was too far off to be reached by the lines so the brigadesmen followed it as it went down the coast, in case it came ashore, until it went over the boundary of their area. It eventually stranded at Seaham and the Seaham VLB attended to rescue the crew. At their second attempt with the rocket and line it became tangled with the bowsprit and one of the ship's crew, George Foster, bravely climbed along and retrieved the line, putting his own life at risk. Two of the crew were landed but then the third, an apprentice Edward Packman, was unfortunately either washed out of, or slipped from, the breeches buoy when about halfway between the ship and the shore. Despite his own efforts to get ashore he was swept away. A further four crew members were then successfully rescued. The names of the crew were Frederick Flint (master), Samuel Flick, John Crump, George Hentage, George Forster and another apprentice named Shilling.[7]

The final call out that night was at the north pier where the schooner *Golden Light* became stranded on the bar, but this ship was hauled off by a steam tug so the apparatus was not

Right: John W. Broderick, honorary secretary of Sunderland Volunteer Life Brigade for many years.

Below: The *J.B. Eminson*, wrecked February 1881.

Throwing the heaving cane in a drill.

needed.[8] By 10.00 a.m. the next day it was reported that the storm was abating, but this did not prevent the brigantine *Rapid* being dismasted; and, although the brigade was called out to stand by, the ship was towed ashore and the crew jumped to safety onto the pier.[9]

That winter was one of the most eventful for the brigade, with further action after the New Year when the ketch *Rising Sun* was driven ashore behind the north pier in a heavy sea and snow squalls. Her crew managed to jump ashore before the brigade reached them. On 5 February 1881, the SS *Broomhill* struck the bar and drove onto rocks; the apparatus was launched by the brigade but the rescue was made by the lifeboat.

A strong southerly gale was blowing on 7 February 1881 when the *J.B. Eminson*, a Sunderland registered iron steamship, was sailing from London to the Wear in ballast. She attempted to enter the river that evening at about 8.00 p.m. when the sea was heaving. She grounded very close to the north pier. Both divisions of the VLB were called out, the Roker division getting a line on board the vessel by means of a heaving cane.

The heaving cane was a short length of cane with lead in one end and a leather loop at the other; a light line would be attached to the loop. These were used when a ship was very close to the shore. The South division then fired a rocket, but unfortunately this missed. The Roker division rescued one crew member by breeches buoy. The rest of the crew of sixteen managed to get onto the pier by using a ladder, showing how close the ship was to it. Several steam tugs tried to tow the stranded vessel off the rocks but the vessel became a total loss; parts of the wreck can occasionally be seen at very low spring tide.

During this period, the organisation of the brigade was changing. Set up originally as one brigade with two divisions, it was found that this caused some complications. Initially it had been intended that brigadesmen could man any of the sets of rocket apparatus placed in their area. Inevitably it was found that those who lived south of the river were principally interested in serving on rescues in that area and similarly with those who lived at Roker and Monkwearmouth in the north.

In 1881 an agreement was reached by which the two divisions became separate units, each with its own finances and managing its own affairs. Retaining the structure of three companies in the south and two in the north, the Sunderland South brigade was allocated three fifths of income from the Board of Trade and money raised by donation and subscription, and the Roker brigade the remaining two thirds. They became known as the Sunderland VLB and Roker VLB respectively. Although separate organisations, the two brigades did come together for some fundraising events and also where joint celebrations were appropriate.

Gladys

Between the hours of 10.00 p.m. and 11.00 p.m. on 4 December 1882, the screw steamer *Gladys* of Whitby arrived off the port and signalled for the pilot to go out to take her in. The heavy seas meant that no pilot could go and the ship's master, Captain McGregor, not wanting to risk a strange harbour in the dark and storm, put out to sea again. By the following morning there were reports of very high seas and blinding showers of sleet and hailstones. Shortly after 5.00 a.m. a huge wave struck the vessel with such force that her starboard bow was stoved in and the captain at once tried to make for the safety of Sunderland harbour.

At 6.30 a.m. the signals were fired to call out the brigade and a number ran to get out the equipment. The *Gladys* was being driven ashore by the storm and the rocket apparatus was carried near to her, but she came so close to a jetty that lines could be thrown to her. These were used to take off the twenty-three crew members and the son of the owner, Mr Marwood, all of whom were exhausted.

Captain Hooper of the coastguard took Captain McGregor and Mr Marwood to his home to recover from their ordeal, and the rest of the crew were taken to the brigade watch house where they were quickly given hot drinks. During the morning the vessel was further damaged with her stern post and rudder being broken, and it seemed that she would be completely wrecked.[10]

Grinkle

This was a cargo ship that was being used to carry iron ore to Jarrow on the Tyne for industry. The *Grinkle* had left the River Tyne on the evening of 15 October 1883, bound for Rosedale, when at about 8.00 p.m. a strong wind began to blow and there were heavy seas off the north-east coast. Shortly afterwards she struck Hendon Rock with her bow and water started to rush in. Captain Varl turned the vessel to head back to the Tyne but the water gained rapidly and soon put out her fires. She was then headed towards the Wear, but with the engines stopped she was left to the mercy of the waves. It seemed at first that she would make it to harbour, but she was dashed against the end of the pier. An attempt was made to pull her around into the harbour by using hawsers but this was unsuccessful and she was carried on to the shore.

The brigade passed life lines to the crew and all ten were quickly rescued. They were taken to the brigade watch house and given refreshments and accommodated for the night in the bunk room. Later that day the *Grinkle* was reported to be lying with her head to the shore, her keel and stem were torn and her rudder bent. Some of her ropes and stores were taken ashore but it was expected that she would flood with the rising tide.[11]

Sleipner

The *Sleipner* was a Norwegian brigantine carrying pit props to the port of Sunderland when, on 16 February 1884, she went aground on the north sands just after 6.30 a.m. The coastguard and brigadesmen on watch were soon on the scene and the signal rockets were fired to summon others. There were eight crewmen on board the ship and the brigade quickly fired a rocket and line to them, but at first they did not know how to secure it. Eventually the line was properly fastened and, after half an hour, all the crew were brought ashore and taken to the watch house.

They were soaked through and their rescuers were unable to provide them with dry clothing as there was a lack of supplies. The brigade appealed through the local press for clean cast-off clothing to be kept in store. The brigadesmen were led on the rescue by Captains John Barlow, William Milburn, Robert Swan and John Pearce. The beautifully carved name board of the *Sleipner* is still on display in Roker Watch House.

In the first twenty years of the service, the Sunderland brigade was called out fifty-seven times, an average of almost three times a year. There were some years, however, when there was a much greater demand than others. The rescues that took place during the great storm of 1880 have already been commented on and a similar year was 1885 with nine call outs for the brigade, seven of which were in the first three months of the year. The first was on 3 January, when the SS *Dolphin* struck the bar and ran up against the north pier – one member of the crew was taken off with the apparatus before the ship managed to get into harbour where she capsized.

Olivia

Thirteen days later the schooner *Olivia* grounded on the bar. The brigade, responding to the distress signal, put a line on board but the apparatus would not function due to the way in which the line had been secured on the ship. One of the rescuers, coastguardsman Drew, volunteered to go hand over hand across the hawser to the ship to free the line. Once he had freed the apparatus the entire crew of five were rescued; Drew was the last man to leave the ship.

A Complaint against the Brigade

It was the master of the *Olivia* who wrote to the local press in support of the brigade after a complaint had been made by the crew of the *Lady Ann Duff*. This followed the death of two members of her crew when the vessel was wrecked at the south entrance to the harbour on 17 January 1885.[12] The two surviving crew members complained that, after they got ashore, they found brigadesmen in the watch house in front of the fire and not attempting a rescue.[13]

The inquest into the deaths of two crew members, held on 19 January, heard that the ship's master, who was one of the deceased, mistook the lights of a steamer for the harbour entrance. The ship was driven ashore and two of the crew managed to jump onto the pier. The apparent assumption that the volunteers of the brigade had failed to do their duty was taken up robustly by the local press, with a leader written in the *Sunderland Daily Echo*. This strongly worded piece compared signing a cheque or giving a donation with the unselfish and self-sacrificing actions of the volunteers.[14]

In fact the brigade had, earlier in the night, rescued the crew of the *Olivia* and then gone back on watch. They were called out again at 4.30 a.m. when a flare was seen but the whereabouts of the ship could not be ascertained due to the darkness. As soon as the two survivors gave an indication of where this ship, the *Lady Ann Duff*, had struck they went there but there was nothing to be seen, the ship having quickly broken up. Captain Hooper of the coastguard was very clear that there were no brigadesmen in the watch house at the time stated and that the brigade had been ready for action.[15]

Name board of the *Sleipner* on display in the watch house.

The old Sunderland South Pier Lighthouse. (By kind permission of Sunderland Antiquarian Society)

William Milburn, captain of Sunderland Volunteer Life Brigade for many years.

The apparent mystery was clarified the following day when a letter from Captain William Callum, the master of the *Olivia*, was published. In it he stated that it was he and his crew who were in the watch house warming by the fire and whom the survivors from the *Lady Ann Duff* had seen. He also confirmed that no brigadesmen had been there for at least half an hour before the other crew arrived. He also took the opportunity to thank the brigade for their care and for housing his crew for two days until arrangements could be made for their passage home.[16]

On 17 January 1885 the brigade were called out to attend the SS *Faraday* which had collided with the end of the south pier.[17] The same day the barque *Bedfordshire* drove against the north pier and then onto the beach. Two companies were called out under the command of Captains Barlow and Milburn and Deputy Captains Swan and Pearce. The crew of seven men were landed safely by the breeches buoy, although the master at that stage refused to leave. The ship later became a total wreck.[18] This was another of several incidents where large crowds, gathering to view the wreck, hindered the actions of the brigade. This appears to have been a frequent occurrence that dogged the operations of brigades from their early days.

Gwendoline

The *Gwendoline* was a Middlesbrough steamer bound from Erith to Sunderland in ballast on 20 February 1888. As the vessel approached the harbour entrance with waves breaking heavily she seemed to be dangerously near to the north pier. A strong current in the ebb tide then carried her onto the pier. Her stem was broken off and she was washed around the pier then grounded a couple of hundred yards from it. The members of the VLB, who had been constantly on watch during the storm, were mustered and soon got a line to the steamer. Captain John Barlow led the rescuers who, with the breeches buoy equipment, landed eleven people. The master, Captain Leader, the chief engineer and the mate remained on board for some time longer. The crew were taken to the watch house where they were looked after. Many hundreds of people visited the scene of the incident during that day.

The SS *Harraton*, which was also driven against the north pier on 22 February, managed to get into harbour before a rescue was needed, and on 1 March the brigade, with the rocket apparatus, landed eight people from the schooner *James*, including three pilots who had gone on board to give assistance.

George Soulsby

On 6 August 1888, George Soulsby, along with other members of Sunderland VLB, attended the unveiling of a memorial to Sunderland hero Jack Crawford. On their return to the watch house after the ceremony they heard cries for help coming from the dock. A boy, Francis Renton, had been playing near the quay steps and had slipped into the water. He was eight years old and the son of Frank Renton, a blacksmith, of Thomas Street. Francis was in imminent danger of drowning so George Soulsby immediately jumped into the water. Despite being severely hampered by his heavy clothing he managed to reach the boy. He then grabbed him and swam to nearby steps. Others assisted them out of the water and some took the boy home. George returned to the watch house to change his clothing.

This was reported to be Soulsby's sixth rescue of a person from drowning.[19] He was awarded the Royal Humane Society's Testimonial on Vellum for his actions. George Soulsby was forty years old at the time of this rescue and he was a Sunderland man. He was a painter by trade and lived in East Woodbine Street, Hendon with his wife Margaret and their children Edith, Lillian, George and William.

1888 *Bon Accord*

At about 8.20 p.m. on 6 November 1888 the sound of the signal guns alerted that a ship was in distress near Sunderland harbour. The *Bon Accord* had attempted to enter when the tide was low and had struck the bar. Attempts were made to get her off but when a heavy sea struck she did not answer her helm and drifted close to the north pier. The tide was ebbing, which caused her to ground and she was hard fast. The Roker division of the VLB had been on watch near the

Memento of the *Harraton* below that of the *Arbutus* in the watch house.

A group of River Wear pilots. (By kind permission of Sunderland Antiquarian Society)

Five members of Sunderland Volunteer Life Brigade. (George Soulsby is second from the right)

John Barlow.

pier and had seen the vessel, immediately sending word to the coastguard to sound the signal. The brigadesmen, under command of Captains Barlow and Milburn, were soon at the scene and a rocket fired to the ship. The hawser was attached to the ship's foremast and the breeches buoy sent across, spinning in the wind.

The crew of eight men were landed on the pier safely but the captain, named Talbot, stayed with his vessel hoping that it could be refloated at high water. Although not recorded, it is highly probable that some of the brigadesmen stood watch over the ship during the night in case the captain needed to be taken off. The crew were taken to the watch house and warmed themselves in front of a good fire. They were given warm drinks and in all likelihood dry clothing, and spent the night in the watch house.

The following day it was reported that the *Bon Accord* had begun to break up in heavy seas, and that by 3.00 a.m. she had broken in two. Luckily the coastguard had persuaded Captain Talbot to leave the vessel shortly before she broke up, when it was clear that his life was in great

SS *Ottercaps*, wrecked August 1890.

John Herring's sketch of the wreck of the *Jaenaes*. (By kind permission of Anne Williams and John Dale)

danger. The crew applied to the Shipwrecked Mariner's Society to be helped in returning to their home port of Aberdeen.

The number of call outs to the brigade, and the number of rescues that were attempted, varied greatly according to the time of year and prevailing conditions. The majority of casualties took place from the beginning of October to the end of February, as expected, when the winter months brought high winds and storms. Between the years 1877 – 1900 only one rescue took place in the summer months.

Ottercaps

At about 10.45 p.m. on 10 August 1890, chief officer W. Thompson of the coastguard saw the light of a steamer dangerously close to the shore and heard her bump on the rocks. The man on watch, William Batchelor, called the coastguards while Captain Thompson discharged the signal rockets to call the VLB. These were six sound rockets, in pairs, at intervals of a minute each. Six coastguards and fifty-two brigadesmen answered the summons with VLB Captain Ridley and Deputy Captains Herbert and Wilkinson.

The ship was identified as a well-known vessel on the Wear, the *Ottercaps*, captained by Allan B. Watts. The ship was bound to Sunderland from London in water ballast and had a crew of sixteen, as well as two passengers on board. In attempting to make the harbour in a heavy sea and rain, the *Ottercaps* missed the entrance and drove ashore about 200yds south of the south pier.

The rocket apparatus was used to fire a line to the ship and the first person to be rescued was the wife of the engineer. After this was a boy of about four or five years of age, the son of one of the crew. Thirteen of the crew and the two passengers were all landed within twenty-five minutes but the captain, chief officer and steward declined to leave until the vessel was left dry by the tide. The crew were taken to the watch house for hot drinks and dry clothing.[20] The engineer's wife, Mrs A. Robinson, was taken to the home of Captain Thompson to be looked after, and she later wrote a letter to the local press thanking all those involved in the rescue.[21]

The press reports stated that thousands of people, on hearing the signal guns, went to see the sight and their numbers were so great that they hampered the work of the rescuers. The brigadesmen reported that many were drunk and ill-behaved. The next morning the *Ottercaps* was lying high on the sands with her sternpost and rudder damaged but, as the weather had eased, it was hoped that she could soon be refloated.

Local Hero – John Leviss

During the long history of Sunderland VLB only one brigadesman has lost his life in the course of duty. On 21 October 1894 the Norwegian barque *Jaenaes* attempted to make the harbour at low water to land a sick man, but she missed and drove ashore on Hendon beach. Distress signals were seen at about noon and, as usual, drawn by the signal, hundreds of local people went to the shore to witness the event.

The brigade was called out as the sea was running very high and about thirty brigadesmen attended. The volunteers had to follow the ship along the coast until they were in a position to fire a line to her. The size of the crowd, that had again gathered to watch the rescue, was so large that it hampered the work of the brigade and made their work hazardous. The line to the ship was secured and five crew members were taken off by breeches buoy, with four others getting ashore on a boat.

Owing to the crowd, the brigadesmen were working in a very confined space and one man, John Leviss, was on the breakwater. Appeals were made to the crowd to stand back but they encroached until the men had only a few feet to work in. A heavy sea then struck the ship causing it to move and the communicating line to jerk. Leviss, and some other men, were standing in the bight of the line which was pulled tight knocking them off their feet. All got up except Leviss who, still clinging to the rope, was flung over the sea wall.

The sea was too high for anyone to go in after him and ropes were thrown but it was half an hour before he was dragged clear and onto the pier; the line was caught around his neck and body.[22] One of the doctors present, Dr Wood, tried for some time to revive Leviss without success and he concluded that his death was due to drowning.

John Leviss was in his thirties and had been employed as a carter for a local miller. He left a widow, Jane Ann; three young children, John, Jane and Isabella; and Ernest Trott, the adopted child of a relative. The main cause of the tragedy was deemed to be the difficulty caused by the press of the crowd interfering in the work of the brigadesmen and the coroner's jury suggested that the police should attend whenever a wreck occurred to keep control of the crowds.[23] One of the rescued seamen later died in Sunderland infirmary and it transpired that the captain had been trying to reach shore to land this man when the wreck occurred.[24]

John Leviss was buried a few days later and crowds lined the route from his home in Woodbine Street to the cemetery. Some thirty members of the Sunderland South brigade accompanied his coffin, which was carried on the rocket cart and covered with the Union Flag. Also in attendance were thirty men from the Roker brigade and representatives of the coastguard and naval reserve. Other VLBs were represented by fifty men from the South Shields brigade, ten from Tynemouth and ten from Whitburn Life Saving Company. A fund was set up immediately to provide relief for Leviss's family and £700 was raised and placed in a trust fund. Thereafter, for many years the fund paid about £1 per week to support Mrs Leviss and her family.

Resolue

November 1897 saw some very stormy weather which meant that the brigadesmen were keeping a close watch for any signs of a ship in danger. The storms raged across the eastern coast of England on the 29th of that month and much damage was done. In Sunderland, the flagstaff at St John's Church was snapped off, railway gates wrecked and trees were uprooted. At Tynemouth, part of the north pier was washed away. Between fifty and sixty lives were lost at sea off the coast, but at least 136 lives were saved by lifeboats and rocket apparatus.

Right: John Leviss. (By kind permission of Howard Glansfield)

Below: John Herring's sketch of an unknown ship in a storm. (By kind permission of Anne Williams and John Dale)

The original wreck board on which all rescues
were recorded.

It was in this storm that the schooner *Resolue* came to grief in a gale with fierce squalls of sleet and snow. She was seen in distress and drifting towards the shore. The coastguard summoned the brigade and as soon as the ship seemed to be within range they fired a rocket to her. The first fell short but the second was on target and the line was secured by the crew. By this time the gale was at its height and the waves were pounding both the vessel and the shore. The coastguards and the brigadesmen were at times working up to their waists in the sea.

The first person to be brought ashore was, unusually, the master as he was ill but, while he was in transit, a line on the apparatus failed and the master and breeches buoy were dropped into the sea. On seeing this, two men performed an act of great bravery. Coastguardsman Hodge and brigadesman Payne, who had been standing by to receive the crew, went into the sea without hesitation. One of them fixed the line while the other supported the master in the breeches buoy and assisted him to land. This action not only saved the life of the master but also of the rest of the crew, as there was no delay in getting the remaining five crew members ashore. As the last man was being landed, the *Resolue* turned over and broke into pieces. Hodge and Payne were both awarded medals for their gallantry.

Notes

1 G. Patterson, '*Victorian Working Life*', in G.E. Milburn & S.T. Miller (eds) *Sunderland River, Town and People* (Sunderland: Sunderland Borough Council, 1990), pp. 51–2

2 *Sunderland Daily Echo*, 15 October 1877, p. 3

3 Letter of Henry Broomfield, survivor, written to *Sunderland Daily Echo* 25 March 1927

4 *Sunderland Daily Echo*, 28 October 1880, p. 3

5 *Sunderland Daily Echo*, 30 April 1878, p. 3

6 *YMCA Flashes*, Vol. 13 No. 147, November 1905.

7 *Sunderland Daily Echo*, 29 October 1880, p. 3

8 Ibid.

9 *Sunderland Daily Echo*, 30 October 1880, p. 3

10 *Sunderland Daily Echo*, 5 December 1882, p. 3

11 *Sunderland Daily Echo*, 16 October 1883, p. 3

12 *Sunderland Daily Echo*, 21 January 1885, p. 2

13 *Sunderland Daily Echo*, 19 January 1885, p. 3

14 *Sunderland Daily Echo*, 20 January 1885, p. 2

15 *Sunderland Daily Echo*, 20 January 1885, p. 2

16 *Sunderland Daily Echo*, 21 January 1885, p. 2

17 *Sunderland Daily Echo*, 19 January 1885, p. 3

18 Ibid.

19 *Sunderland Daily Echo*, 6 August 1888, p. 3

20 *Sunderland Daily Echo*, 11 August 1890, p. 3

21 *Sunderland Daily Echo*, 12 August 1890, p. 3

22 *Sunderland Daily Echo*, 22 October 1894, p. 3

23 *Sunderland Daily Echo*, 23 October 1894, p. 3

24 *Sunderland Daily Echo*, 22 October 1894, p. 3

five

MANAGING THE WORK

Equipment

The rocket apparatus used by Sunderland VLB in rescuing seamen was provided by the responsible Government department, the Board of Trade. Although there were several improvements and developments in equipment, the basic method changed little over the years.

VLBs have only ever used shore-based rescue equipment, rather than venturing to sea in boats – this was the province of lifeboat men. The coastguard were responsible for shore-based lifesaving and it was to assist in their work that the brigades were set up. When a ship in distress was spotted and it was deemed necessary for the VLB to be called out, a signal was sounded. The Board of Trade initially gave the use of three thirty-two pounder guns for this purpose, although these were replaced within a few years by signal rockets. In the days before widespread use of telephones and the invention of pagers, this was the most effective means of summoning the volunteers.

Most brigadesmen lived and worked close to their watch house and equipment stations and would be prepared to leave their homes, beds or work when a call out happened. Local firms were supportive of the brigades in allowing their brigadesmen employees to leave work in order to attend call outs.

An initial assessment of the situation would be made by the commanding officer of the coastguard and, hopefully, the location of the ship would be determined. In the dark winter nights, however, it was not always easy to determine the exact location of a ship that had fired distress signals and there were no strong searchlights to assist. Quite often, the brigadesmen had to get their apparatus ready and then stand by until the ship was located or it was in a position, relatively close to the shore, where they could use the rocket effectively.

In 1877, the year that Sunderland VLB was founded, the Board of Trade issued four-wheeled carts to transport the breeches buoy rocket equipment. At the same time, they issued a printed list of the equipment, official document number LSA (Life Saving Apparatus) 25, which was to be kept in the cart. The cart could be pulled either by horses or men and there were many

Rocket cart.

Sunderland Volunteer Life Brigade cliff-rescue training, 1980s.

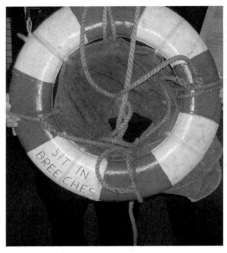

Above: Breeches buoy on display at the watch house.

Left: Showing the instruction to sit in the breeches buoy.

incidents where the brigadesmen had to manhandle the cart over rough terrain to get near the site of a wreck.

Once the best place to set up the equipment was determined, a rocket with a light line attached would be fired over to the ship. The rocket launcher was set up as near to being vertical as possible by using a plumb weight. This was to ensure that the rocket reached its optimum range. In stormy weather with gale force winds, and with only eyesight to determine the range and angle for the rocket, the brigade's skill and experience was key if they were to get the first rocket onto the ship.

Once the line was taken aboard, the crew would signal to the shore and then haul over a pulley block with a line, the whip line, rove through it. The whip is a long length of heavier line with the ends joined. The block had to be made fast to the ship, in a high position so that the lines would not foul on any part of the structure. A hawser was then sent over to the ship by the brigadesmen which was made fast to the same point as the block but above it. Again the crew would signal that the equipment was in place and then the brigadesmen would tighten the hawser and, using the whip line, would send over to the ship the breeches buoy into which the first person to be rescued would sit.

The brigadesmen would then pull the breeches buoy with its occupant over to the shore, assist the person out and then haul the empty breeches buoy back to the ship. This would be repeated over and over again until all the passengers and crew were landed. Finally, the hawser would be cut, allowing some of the equipment to be retrieved for future use. Detailed and very clear instructions on the use of the rocket apparatus were issued by the Board of Trade and the brigadesmen were regularly drilled in its use so that they were ready for action when the need arose.

As well as instructing the brigadesmen, the crews of ships also had to be alerted to the means of rescue. When the apparatus was used, a tally board was sent over to the ship with the first line giving instructions to the crew of how to fasten the line. The instructions were written in several languages so that they could be read by a large number of foreign crews, but inevitably

Above: Belts and armbands worn as part of the uniform. The captains wore the belt with a crown.

Right: Unknown brigadesman wearing original gansey.

there were times when crews in distress were either unable to attach the lines properly or the conditions made this very difficult.

The stories of the rescues show several occasions when brigadesmen or coastguards, often in great peril, climbed along the line to a ship to help secure the apparatus and assist the crew in leaving. Gradually more precise instructions were published and distributed widely to crews of vessels using the ports of Great Britain.

The brigadesmen all wore uniform when active, either at drills or rescues, which helped to identify them and their role. Initially the uniform was a navy blue gansey – a thick knitted woollen jumper – embroidered with the brigade's name, as well as caps similar to those worn by sailors. Belts and armbands were issued by the Board of Trade.

Oilskins were later also purchased and issued for wet-weather watches and for the rescues. The difficulties of working in what would be very restrictive clothing can only be imagined, especially when rain and spray from the sea would soon soak through, making them heavy to

Search and rescue team in modern gear.

wear. The search and rescue service, run by the modern Sunderland VLB, has special equipment and safety clothing designed both to protect the wearer and to be easy to use, but as recently as the last breeches buoy rescue in 1963 the newsreel clearly shows the rescuers wearing older style uniforms.

The care and maintenance of the equipment used in rescues cannot be underestimated and this is as true today as it was in the early days of lifesaving. When the gear was stored after a drill or a rescue it had to be cleaned, dried and left so that it could be quickly used again. No matter how tired or wet the brigadesmen were, they knew that their lives and the lives of others depended on safe and usable equipment being at the ready.

The cliff-rescue equipment used by the modern search and rescue team requires equal care and maintenance, with ropes being regularly checked for any signs of wear. When a colleague is being lowered down a cliff face there needs to be absolute confidence in the safety of the gear.

From the earliest days, the brigadesmen were trained in first aid, with many attaining certificates from the St John's Ambulance Association. Swimming classes were also given at one time.

The Brigadesmen

The records of the brigade give little insight into the lives of the brigadesmen. Few records have survived of members until modern recording was started. Reports of rescues usually only mention the names of those in command: the captains and deputy captains. Occasionally, when an heroic act took place or disciplinary action was taken, the names of ordinary brigadesmen were recorded. Some accounts of those who attended the regular training drills survive, but often they give only a surname and initial. There is only one surviving record of members from Sunderland South, most relate to the men at Roker.

A record of drills by the Roker brigade from 1895 gives a little more detail and this highlights the sense of community that must have existed. Of the fifty-two members whose addresses were given, or which have been traced, forty-nine men lived within twenty-four streets in the Roker and Monkwearmouth areas, and twenty-nine of these lived within eight streets. Most of the brigadesmen were, therefore, fairly close neighbours who would have known one another. This appears to show a tightly knit community which was probably mutually supportive but, in addition to this, it is certain that many of the men also knew one another through their work environments.

It has been possible using this record and census returns to identify the occupations of thirty-nine of the fifty-five men listed. As may be envisaged, in a large industrial port twenty-nine of the men were employed in shipbuilding or related industries. The range of occupations is interesting in that it is clear that people from a wide range of backgrounds had volunteered for the service, as included in the list are several men who would be classed as being from a professional or managerial background.

Four of these were from the same family, the Barlows: John Barlow senior and his four sons John, Robert, Thomas and Joseph. In addition, Robert Dring is described as a manager; there is a local chemist, Ernest Cherett; and the Bairds, who were boat builders. The diversity of occupations is further shown by the inclusion of a local hairdresser, Thomas Wellburn, a showman Walter Johnson and the licensee of the Mount Pleasant Inn, Robert Watts.

It was not uncommon for men from the same family to serve together in the brigade. As well as the Barlow family, there was another case of a father and sons volunteering together: the Albion family. Henry Albion was born around 1860 and joined the brigade around 1897. He eventually became the captain of No.1 Company and served until 1935 when he went onto the Honorary List. His sons, John William and Henry, joined up in 1907 to be followed later by their younger brothers George and Fred. There were also many examples of brothers serving together.

The brigadesmen often took part in local events in the town, including parades and processions. In 1910 they took part in the procession held in the town to mark the funeral of King Edward VII.

Long service within the brigade was not unusual. A great many men received awards for long service, that being more than twenty years, and a lot of men served much longer. Robert Dring joined the brigade in 1884 and achieved fifty years of service. This occasion was marked with the unveiling of a photograph of him in the watch house in January 1934.

Social events were often held and most of these in the early brigade were solely for the brigadesmen and, only very occasionally, their wives. Concerts were held, whist drives and darts matches. In more recent years family parties have been held in the watch houses at Christmas and on brigade occasions, and an annual trip used to be run.

Four members of the Albion family.

Robert Dring as a young brigadesman.

Sunderland Volunteer Life Brigade in procession, marking the death of King Edward VII, 1910.

A family party at the Roker Watch House.

Visiting the watch house.

The Watch Houses

The watch houses, one on each side of the River Wear, were essential to the work of the brigade and they were used for several purposes. They provided a base and a training venue; they were used to look out over the harbour to keep watch for ships in distress; and they also provided accommodation for shipwrecked crews. The current Roker Watch House was built with a bunk room, now used as a committee room, which was lined with tiers of bunks to accommodate up to twenty-three people. There was a stove in the main hall to provide warm meals and hot drinks.

Although some of the crews using the port were local, Sunderland was an international trading port and many shipwrecked sailors needed to be housed and fed until they could return to their home port or find another ship. Although there were several Missions to Seamen in the town that provided accommodation, it was to the watch houses that the rescued sailors would go for immediate care and comfort. No additional financing was received for providing these comforts and the brigade frequently made appeals for good, clean unwanted clothing from the public in order to meet this need.

Alongside the watch houses were the cart houses. These were built to house the rocket equipment and other gear used during the rescues, as well as the carts used to carry them. As explosives were used to fire the rockets, the Board of Trade set out strict guidelines for the construction and fitting out of the cart houses.

Shortly after the Sunderland VLB was founded in 1877, the Board of Trade financed the building of a watch house for the South division, but there was no similar help for the Roker division. The RWC did grant the Roker brigade the use of a small building, but initially the men kept watch outside in all weathers.

The second Roker Watch House was purpose-built on land donated by the North Eastern Railway and work began in 1879. As there was no funding, the brigade relied on donations of money, goods and labour to build and furnish the house. It was not fully completed until February 1881. This house had a lookout on the first floor for the men to keep watch and was fitted with bunks so that rescued seamen could be accommodated overnight. Unfortunately, by 1885 the RWC decided that they needed the land and a third watch house had to be provided.

The foundation stone for this house was laid on 23 September 1885 on a site further to the east and on the north pier. The RWC provided funding for the shell of the building, but all the fitting out and equipment was again funded by donations. This watch house was in use for twenty years until being replaced by the current building.

In 1905 land was acquired for a new Roker Watch House; the old building was sold to the RWC and work started to raise funds for the building. One of the captains of the brigade, a builder by trade, Robert Swan, was responsible for the building of this watch house with many of the members providing help. The cost of the building was £600 with a further £200 for furnishings and, as in the past, this was raised by the brigade itself.

Over £400 was contributed by public donations and there were many generous gifts of materials. The opening ceremony took place on 7 February 1906. As well as the main hall, a bunk room was included and this remained until 1986 when its use was changed to a committee room. The building is still in use and has changed little from its early days. The lookout, today used by the Coastwatch, provided an ideal vantage point for spotting ships in distress.

Right: The Cart House built to house the rescue apparatus.

Below: Roker Watch House, built 1881.

Plate from a dinner service used in the watch house.

Mug from a dinner service used in the watch house (front).

Mug from a dinner service used in the watch house (back).

Roker Watch House, opened 1906.

The Southside brigade also had several watch houses. The first one was on land behind the south pier but it does not appear to have been in use for very long as an application was made in 1879 for land for a new building, and an agreement was reached for this to be sited near the coastguard houses at the south pier. This second watch house was opened in March of that year. An addition was made to the building in 1885, considerably increasing its size, and this was built by a brigadesman, Mr T. Cole. About seventy officers and men attended a supper held to mark its opening on 18 March.[1]

The conclusion of the building of a new south pier in 1912 brought a problem for the Sunderland South brigade as their outlook to sea was blocked by the pier works. It was decided that a new building was needed. The Board of Trade contributed half of the estimated cost of £500 and the RWC gave a site at the end of the new pier. An appeal was made to the public to raise the rest of the cost of the building and this was supported by Samuel Storey who, as mayor, had helped to set up the brigade.

Robert Swan.   John Bell Wilkinson.

Storey stated in the press that once £200 had been raised then he would donate the final £50 needed. A good description of the building, which was constructed by the local firm of D&J Ranken, was given in the *Sunderland Echo*. It was made of red brick, stood twenty-eight feet high and had a flat roof that could be used as a lookout. There was a large double door leading to a main room where the equipment was to be kept and a large upstairs room with a bay window to be used by the men on watch. It was fitted with an ingenious ventilation system designed by VLB Captain John Bell Wilkinson.[2]

John Bell Wilkinson

John Bell Wilkinson was a member of a Sunderland family, although he was born in London on 8 February 1847. His parents were Bell and Mary Wilkinson. In 1861 he was living with his parents in Stepney and was described as a plumber, presumably an apprentice. About 1867 he moved to Sunderland, living for some time with his uncle Yeal Wilkinson. He married Louisa Ellen Lynn in 1872 in Middlesex and they were living in Sunderland in 1881, where he was a plumber employing five men and four apprentices. He set up his business in Bedford Street and Sunderland remained his home for the rest of his life.

In 1922 John was elected the Master of the Worshipful Company of Plumbers, one of the oldest of the London guilds. He was also made a Freeman of the City of London. He was one of the first members of Sunderland Liberal Club, of which he became chairman, and he served for a time on the town council.

Sunderland South Watch House, opened 1912.

John was a founder member of Sunderland VLB and he attended the very first meeting held in 1877. He served as captain of one of the Sunderland South companies for many years and was senior captain and honorary treasurer at the time of his death. In 1927 he celebrated his 80th birthday and a social evening was held by the brigade to mark this, and also his long service. On this occasion he presented a framed photograph of himself to hang in the brigade house, which is now in the Roker Watch House.

John Wilkinson died on 20 February 1929 at his home in Park Road. His funeral was held three days later and his coffin was borne into St John's Church through two ranks of brigadesmen. It was draped with the Union Flag and on it was his VLB cap and belt. Six brigadesmen acted as bearers. As a mark of the respect in which he was held, detachments of both divisions of the VLB followed his coffin. The officers present were Captains R.M. Price, G. Miller and J.J. Wellburn, Honorary Captain Howitt Egglishaw and Deputy Captains G. Gale and C.V. Price.

The new watch house was officially opened on 13 May 1912 when a large marquee was erected nearby to accommodate all those attending. At the same event, several awards were made with Board of Trade Long Service Medals being presented to Captain John Bell Wilkinson, thirty-five years of service; Captain John Herring, also thirty-five years; Dr James W. Beattie, twenty-six years; Joseph Hudson, twenty-six years; Christopher Jackson, twenty-five years and William Woodruff, twenty years.[3] This medal was instituted by the Board of Trade in 1911 to be awarded to those who achieved twenty years' service.

DONATIONS AND SUBSCRIPTIONS, 1878-9.

	£	s.	d.
The Most Noble the Marquis of Londonderry ...	5	0	0
Francis Corder, Esq.	5	0	0
Messrs. Dixon & Wilson	3	3	0
Pearson W. Kidd, Esq.	3	3	0
S. S. Robson, Esq., *Mayor*	3	0	0
Major Duncan, R.A.	2	2	0
Messrs. Peacock Brothers	2	2	0
Edward Backhouse, Esq.	2	0	0
A Friend, per J. J. Kayll, Jun.	1	1	0
Henry Ritson, Esq.	1	1	0
James Westoll, Esq.	1	1	0
Capt. T. B. Taylor	1	1	0
J. W. Wayman, Esq.	1	1	0
Henry Tonkinson, Esq.	1	1	0
Thos. C. Stamp, Esq.	1	1	0
W. B. Hopper, Esq.	1	1	0
Wm. St. John, Esq.	1	1	0
Messrs. F. & W. Ritson	1	1	0
Messrs. Freear & Dix	1	1	0
J. T. French, Esq.	1	1	0
S. P. Austin, Esq.	1	1	0
Messrs. Culliford & Clark	1	1	0
Messrs. Turnbull, Son, & Co.	1	1	0
E. C. Robson, Esq.	1	0	0
T. W. Backhouse, Esq.	1	0	0
A. Backhouse, Esq.	1	0	0
J. Christal, Esq.	1	0	0
D. G. Pinkney, Esq.	1	0	0
Alexander Corder, Esq.	1	0	0
Geo. B. Hunter, Esq.	0	10	6
Messrs. S. Fairman & Son	0	10	6
Frederick Gordon, Esq.	0	10	6
Christian Havelock, Esq.	0	10	6
T. M. Watson, Esq.	0	10	6
J. Thompson, Esq.	0	10	6
Messrs. Thomas Elliot & Son	0	10	6
J. F. Marshall, Esq.	0	10	6
Major Reed, S.V.R.C.	0	10	6
J. W. Mounsey, Esq.	0	10	0
Messrs. Jopling & Tuer	0	10	0
J. Taylor, Esq.	0	10	0
Geo. Ryder, Esq.	0	10	0
J. W. Glaholm, Esq.	0	10	0
A. J. Moore, Esq.	0	10	0
J. Firth, Esq.	0	5	0
J. H. Watson, Esq.	0	5	0
W. O. Whinham, Esq.	0	5	0

Part of a list of subscriptions and donations 1878-9.

74

Model of Sunderland Volunteer Life Brigade Land Rover.

An article in the *Sunderland Daily Echo* in December 1913 describes the cosiness of the new Southside Watch House when an annual supper was held there. It describes the wreck board, now in the Roker Watch House, that chronicled the rescues achieved by the brigade since its inception in 1877 and the number of mementoes of these that adorned the walls.[4] This watch house served the Sunderland South brigade until its closure in 1958 when most of the artefacts were moved to Roker.

Fundraising

With very little funding from central government the VLB has always had to raise the funds needed for their watch houses and their equipment. The rocket apparatus used in the rescues, and a cart on which to carry it, was provided by the Board of Trade but everything else had to be acquired. The brigade had a list of subscribers who agreed to contribute an annual amount to the funds, and they also had street collections, collections at football matches and held fundraising events such as whist drives.

There was also a reliance on gifts in kind, particularly when equipping the watch houses and in providing for shipwrecked crews. The accounts for 1878 – 9 show that over £22s' worth of goods were received, including gas pipes and fittings and glass for windows, as well as everyday items such as crockery, books and pictures to make the watch houses more comfortable for the men on watch, and for the comfort of shipwrecked crews who may be accommodated.

New and innovative ways of financing new equipment and providing training are always needed for charities such as the Sunderland VLB, who rely solely on donations and fundraising. The brigade's customised Land Rover, used to carry rescue equipment and to patrol the area, provided an unusual way of doing this. In 2005, a detailed model of the Land Rover in the brigade's livery was produced by Corgi Classic Ltd. The brigade received a number of these to sell to help with fundraising. As a limited edition it was a very popular way of raising cash and also promoting the work of the organisation.

The costs of equipment, training and maintaining the building amount to a considerable sum each year and the brigade continues to raise its own funding. Many charitable organisations have contributed to its upkeep and development through grants and donations. Members organise collections in local shopping areas and at local events. A stall is held at the annual Sunderland Air Show where the brigade also assist by providing some safety cover.

Notes

1 *Sunderland Daily Echo*, 19 March 1885, p.3
2 *Sunderland Daily Echo*, 11 May 1912, p.6
3 *Sunderland Daily Echo*, 13 May 1912, p.4
4 *Sunderland Daily Echo*, 11 December 1913, p.3

six

THE RESCUES 1900–1950

Maliano – The First Rescue of the Twentieth Century

The brigadesmen kept watch all through the winter of 1899-1900 before the signal guns summoned them to a rescue. It was on 23 March 1900 that the Spanish steamer *Maliano* lost steerage and grounded on Roker beach, just 50yds from the pier, and keeled over. A line was fired by the brigadesmen but the breeches buoy could not be used because the crew had not secured the line properly.

One of the coastguards, William Hennen, volunteered to climb the hawser to the ship, a very difficult and dangerous task, which he successfully achieved. The apparatus was made usable and Hennen assisted the twenty-three crew members to safety. The crew were lodged in the watch house overnight and given dry clothing and refreshments. To commemorate their rescue, some of the crew had a photograph taken of themselves with the brigadesmen and they presented a copy to the brigade. William Hennen was awarded the Board of Trade Sea Gallantry Medal for his part in the rescue.

The Great Storm of 1901

On 11 November 1901 a strong easterly wind started to blow along the east coast, which increased in strength as the hours went by. By the following day, and in the face of the gale, ships were in danger of being blown ashore and would look for shelter, but there were great dangers in trying to enter a harbour. In this era, many ships were still powered only by sail and they were at the mercy of the elements. With the winds reaching force 11, a violent storm rarely experienced, there were many rescues all along the coast and many acts of bravery. By the time the wind subsided four days later, over forty ships had been wrecked on the north-east coast and over 200 sailors had lost their lives. [1]

At Sunderland, the storm brought much damage to buildings. Roofs were blown off, streets were flooded and, at the docks, a large crane was blown into the sea. The situation was bad but

Crew of the *Maliano* with brigadesmen and coastguards.

it was much worse for those who had been caught at sea. The brigadesmen and coastguards were keeping a keen look out for any ships needing assistance. Shortly after noon on 12 November 1901, at the height of the Great Storm, the schooner *Harriot* was spotted off the port of Sunderland in distress. The ship had left Yarmouth for Sunderland two days earlier in fine weather but the storm broke out as she was nearing harbour. In attempting to make the safe haven, the ship was driven past the south pier when, about half a mile out, she grounded.

Two of the crew jumped overboard leaving the captain and mate on board. An attempt was made to take them off but the wind was so strong that the rocket could not reach them. Four times the brigadesmen fired a rocket, but their efforts against the gale were futile. The remaining two men jumped overboard as the waves enveloped their little ship. All four men were pulled from the sea by the rescuers, helped by members of the public who had gathered, some reportedly wading up to their necks in attempting to reach them.

The four men appeared to be lifeless but the captain, Frederick John Bayley, and a young crewman, Thomas Flint, were revived by the attentions of the brigadesmen and Dr Beattie. After two hours of efforts to revive them the mate, Percy Blake, and the other crewman, Frederick Gill, were declared dead. They were aged twenty-two and nineteen years respectively. The local press particularly recorded the efforts of coastguardsmen Balfie and John Hutchinson as well as brigadesmen Burn, Walker, Wilkinson and Oliver. By 2.00 p.m. the *Harriot* had completely broken up with only some wreckage in the sea left.[2]

An inquest was held the following day which the ship's owner, Israel Jackson, attended. The ship's master was unable to attend as he had no clothing or shoes to wear, his own being lost. After hearing evidence from Mr Jackson, the rescuers and Dr Beattie, the deputy coroner, recorded a verdict of accidental drowning and praised the work of the brigade and the coastguard in attempting to save the lives of Blake and Gill. Mr Jackson also gave his thanks and that of the friends and family of the crew.[3]

There was no rest, however, for the men of the brigade and the coastguard as other ships tried for the harbour. Two lucky ones were the *Emily* and the *Cornucopia*, both of Faversham, whose crews managed to get them safely into harbour to the cheers of the watching crowds.[4]

Later that same day at about 4.00 p.m. a small ketch was seen trying to make for Sunderland harbour. The captain made one attempt that failed and then turned to try again. The vessel was near the new south pier when it was hit by heavy seas and driven ashore near the end of the pier. The *Europa* had set sail from Margate the previous Friday, bound for the Wear where she was a frequent visitor. She had lost all her rigging in the storm by the time she arrived off the harbour.

As the vessel was very close to the pier, two of the crew managed to jump from the ship and land safely on it. A third man got ashore with a line that was thrown to him. This left two of the crew still on the ship: Captain John Cook and the cook, Walter Plowman. These men also tried to jump onto the pier but fell into the raging sea and were swept away. The three survivors, Harry Duke, William Cook and one other were taken by the brigadesmen to the watch house where they were looked after with dry clothing, food and hot drinks.[5]

There was no respite for the brigadesmen and coastguards that day for, as well as keeping watch, they were called out for a further time when a barque was seen off the coast. It appeared to be remaining at anchor and weathering the storm. The *Quillotta* had been going from Nantes to Shields in ballast to pick up coal. The storm hit when she was off Sunderland and the captain dropped anchor. The anchor dragged and the ship gradually drifted towards the shore. Occasionally the squalls and spray hid her from sight, but as night fell she was seen off Hendon beach burning distress flares. The conditions were terrible with high winds, driving rain and mountainous seas and it was too rough for the lifeboat to go out.

Hendon beach on a calm day.

The brigade had been standing ready to give assistance and had the rocket apparatus ready, but the conditions were too bad to be able to fire a line successfully. This large ship had stranded a good way out and the brigadesmen could not get nearer to her than about 700yds. The rocket they fired travelled barely half the distance to the ship and, with the tide coming in, they had to retreat. The brigadesmen could see the crew clinging to the lee mizzen rigging, and the lights and distress signals from the ship were visible when a loud report was heard and all the lights disappeared from view.

The *Quillotta* had broken up and her crew of twenty-two were washed into the sea. Two of them, Captain Delepine and seaman Francois Ollivier, were able to reach the shore shortly after the vessel went down. They were found on the beach, cut and bleeding, and were taken to the Toll Bar Inn on Ryhope Road where they were looked after. Shortly after 1.00 a.m. another man, Francois Laignel, was found wandering in Commercial Road, Hendon, with a lifebelt still around him. He was taken, exhausted, to the police station and explained that he had battled for some time against the waves before reaching the shore.

Later a fourth seaman, Ovezeme Le Gorrec, was also found wandering about and he said that he had been washed overboard and tossed around in the sea before eventually thrown onto the shore. He had had to climb the cliffs and he had walked towards the lights of the town. He was found by a man, later identified as James Marman, who took him to his home at 11 Albany Terrace and provided him with food and a bed.

Early the next morning, James Gifford and two friends went along the beach where they saw a man waving from a mound of sand and earth. They went to help and found two men there who had been trying to climb the soft sea bank when it had fallen and buried them. They were both from the *Quillotta*. One of these men had survived the wreck of the ship only to die on shore but the other, named Petit, was taken to a nearby hotel where the brigade's doctor treated him. The remaining seventeen crew were all feared lost but a sixth man, Yves Julon, was discovered much later. He had scrambled along the shore and had been taken to a Seaman's Mission where he stayed overnight. Among the brigade members present at this rescue were Deputy Captains Burns, Wilkinson, and Egglishaw and Mr W.J. Oliver.[6]

Indianic

On 22 November 1904 the *Sunderland Echo* reported the work of the VLB in assisting the crew of the *Indianic*. This ship was a steamer that had been built at J.L. Thompson & Sons Ltd of Sunderland, and was on a voyage from Antwerp in ballast. She had been making little headway in the strong seas and wind and at about 5.00 a.m. she was not answering her helm. The ship was carrying a crew of twenty-five, some of whom were from Sunderland, two passengers and the wife of the second engineer, a Mrs Carter.

The *Indianic* stranded with great force on the rocks south of the south pier but was not visibly damaged and was watertight. The ship had been observed by the men on watch at the Roker Watch House from about 5.20 a.m, and when they saw she was in danger they telegraphed the coastguard station on the south side of the river. The Sunderland South brigade and the coastguard turned out under the command of Chief Officer Parkes, and the first rocket they fired got a line to the ship. The passengers and crew were all safely landed by breeches buoy, although Captain Souter stayed with his vessel. One of the passengers was named as Wilhelm Platz. The other was a fireman who had gained passage on the vessel through the British Consul in Antwerp. They were taken to the coastguard station and given hot drinks and food as well as dry clothing.

It was alleged by some on board that the brigade had been a long time in appearing but it was explained that this was due to the fact that the place the ship stranded was out of view of the coastguard station, but once she was located the rescue had taken place quickly. Along with Chief Officer Parkes were two coastguards, Jones and Smy, and the brigade was in the charge of Captain Burns with Mr Walker and Mr W.J. Oliver also there.

During the rescue, Captain Parkes of the coastguard was washed into the sea and was rescued by two of his colleagues and Mr W.J. Oliver of the brigade. The *Indianic* remained stranded, being lifted higher onto the beach by the storm with her stern resting on the groynes. She was later refloated and taken into Sunderland for repairs.[7]

The following letter was published in the *Sunderland Daily Echo* the day after the rescue:

> Mr and Mrs G. Carter, the second engineer of the *Indianic* and his wife, desire to express their sincere thanks to the Chief Officer of the Coastguards and his staff and to the Sunderland Life Brigade for the valuable services that were rendered to them in connection with the stranding of the steamer yesterday morning.

Sunderland Volunteer Life Brigade outside Sunderland Winter Gardens, *c.*1910.

A Board of Trade inquiry into the stranding of the *Indianic* was opened on 3 January 1905. A representative for the Board of Trade, Mr Burton, told the inquiry that the vessel was owned by the Atlantic Steam Shipping Co. She had left Antwerp on 19 November for Sunderland in water ballast, and due to this she was light in the water. She had encountered fog and so lay at anchor until the following morning when she once more set off. As she approached the north-east coast a gale started to blow, and when she was off Seaham the wind veered and she was caught broadside. At this point she found it hard to make way against the wind and became unmanageable. The wind fell and the crew got her going again. She got near Sunderland when the weather worsened. Her anchors were dropped but failed to hold her. She stranded on the shore and was substantially damaged.

The inquiry lasted for three days and many witnesses were called. There was a suggestion that the captain had been drinking during the voyage and also consideration was given as to whether the vessel was too light. Evidence from the crew and rescuers showed that the captain was not drunk but was more likely to have been suffering from exposure. After much consideration the inquiry concluded that the ship had been properly ballasted and that the captain had taken prompt and proper measures for safety. It also exonerated him from the charge of drunkeness for which he thanked the members of the Board.[8]

Arendal

On 26 March 1906 the *Arendal* was on route from Tonsberg to Sunderland with a cargo of pit props and with eight crewmen on board. She was attempting to enter the port during a north-east gale when she grounded just inside the harbour. The brigade were called out and, with the rocket apparatus, attempted to get a line on board to take off the crew. Unfortunately the ship was too far out for the apparatus to be used and, despite their best efforts, the attempts were unsuccessful. The Sunderland lifeboat attended and took off six of the crew; the captain and first mate decided to stay on board. Later the tugs *Stag* and *Devonia* managed to get lines on board and the *Arendal* was successfully towed into the port.

Orion

On 21 November 1913 the German steamer *Orion* was in passage from Sunderland to Libau with a cargo of 3,000 tons of coal and was leaving the harbour in very heavy seas. She was swept out of the channel and across to the south pier. She struck the bottom and was holed and then driven across the river mouth stranding just inside the north pier. This was very near to where the *J.B. Eminson* had foundered almost thirty years earlier. Tugs and the lifeboat went to assist her.

The VLB was called out as she was sinking fast, but as the lifeboat had reached the vessel they stood by while the crew of nineteen men were taken off. The men were taken to the brigade's watch house by Captains John Herring and J. Walker. A few days later the vessel was reported to be lying with her back broken and with a large crack on her port side; her hull was projecting

The brig *Arendal* being towed into Sunderland harbour, 1906. (By kind permission of Sunderland Antiquarian Society)

The wreck of the *Orion*.

sixty feet out into the river. Attempts were made to salvage her cargo even though she was almost fully submerged at high tide. A total wreck, her broken remains lay with those of the *J.B. Eminson* near the north pier.[9]

Captain John Herring

John Herring was born in September 1858 at 29 Covent Garden Street, Sunderland, his father a sailor. It is known that John joined the Southside division of Sunderland VLB as a founder member, although an exact date of enlistment is not recorded. He served with the brigade for forty-eight years and attained the rank of captain. He was also a member of the Sunderland lifeboat crew and was awarded a certificate of service by the RNLI.

John Herring was a painter and decorator by trade, but he was also an artist who completed several sketch books throughout his life. One sketch book records in some detail several of the early activities of Sunderland VLB, including the visit by the Duke of Edinburgh in 1880, depictions of the use of rocket apparatus and the wreck of the *Jaenaes* when John Leviss lost his life.

John Herring worked mostly in Sunderland but he did travel, being for a time employed in the upkeep of RNLI stations at John O'Groats and in the Orkneys. He was a member of the 7th Durham Volunteers for twenty-one years and retired with the rank of sergeant and a Long Service Medal. He joined the Royal Army Medical Corps during the First World War, when he was in his late fifties, serving for some time in the Sunderland War Hospital. He was awarded a Long Service Medal for his work in the brigade in 1912.

He died on 2 July 1925 at his home in Sunderland and was survived by his widow, Mary Jane, two daughters and a son. His funeral was held on 7 July at Sunderland cemetery where the VLB was represented by Captains Wilkinson, Miller and Price.[10]

The First World War

There is just one recorded rescue that took place during the First World War. Although there are few records from this period, it is certain that the brigade's strength would have been diminished with many of its members being called up or working long hours in occupations vital to the war effort. Those who were available would have taken their turn in providing a watch on Sunderland harbour, ready to raise a signal if a ship was seen that needed assistance.

Geziena

It was about 6.00 a.m. on 6 December 1915 when the brigade was called out to a ship that had gone ashore at the Beacon Rocks, near the south dock. It had been adrift off the coast since the previous day. The vessel was a steel schooner, the *Geziena*, which was bound from Norway to Hartlepool carrying timber. The lifeboat was also called out but could not assist due to shallow water. The coastguards and brigadesmen were helped by soldiers who were stationed at the docks and they soon got a line aboard. The captain, and crew of three, were all taken off with the rocket apparatus.

John Herring, brigadesman and artist. (By kind permission of Anne Williams and John Dale)

The captain, Y.P. Klugkist, had to be forcibly prevented from returning to the ship. He went into the sea in an attempt to get back to her and was restrained by brigadesman J.H. Arrowsmith who went in after him; Captain J.B. Wilkinson assisted with his rescue. All the crew were safely in the watch house by 9.30 a.m. and were given hot drinks.[11] The ship was later reported to have been washed further up the beach, her bottom gone and the cargo of timber able to be seen through the holes.

Solo and *Confield* – October 1919

Gales had been sweeping the coast for several days and the brigade were on watch for casualties when an accident happened near the harbour mouth. It was 30 October and about 6.00 p.m. when the steamers the *Solo* and *Confield* collided. The *Solo* was on her way out of the port laden with coal and bound for France. The *Confield* was in passage to the Wear with a cargo of esparto grass and iron ore. There was no pilot on either ship as there were heavy seas running. The impact between the two was severe and within thirty minutes the lifeboat and the Life Brigade were on stand-by waiting to give assistance should either or both ships succumb.

The *Solo* managed to pull away and was taken back into port by tugs; her bows were very damaged but she was not in danger. The *Confield* was damaged on her port side and the heavy seas and winds drove her across the channel and close to the north pier. She was in serious difficulties and in danger of grounding. The Roker division of the brigade were ready to get a line to her but, with the aid of tugs, she was towed safely back into the harbour and berthed on the river. The brigade and the lifeboat had stood at readiness for about three hours until it was certain that both ships were safe.[12]

Jubilee – the 50th Anniversary Celebrations

March 1927 was the focus for celebrations to mark the 50th anniversary of the founding of Sunderland VLB. Planning for the event began the previous October when a sub-committee was set up to decide on arrangements. This was to be a joint celebration, for both brigades and members were keen to use it to publicise their work and to involve notable people of the town. The date of 23 March was decided on and a programme for the evening put together. After consideration of various venues Mengs restaurant in Fawcett Street, Sunderland was chosen for a dinner and entertainment.

About 124 people attended the celebration including many prominent local businessmen and politicians. As was tradition, a large number of toasts were proposed, including the King, Sunderland VLB and its jubilee, and kindred institutions. After the meal a selection of sea shanties were sung and a number of speeches made.

Appropriately, eight of the original members of the brigade were able to attend. These were John Bell Wilkinson, George T. Stephenson, John Richardson, Thomas Richardson, John Warburton, Robert George Pike, S. Marshall, and J.T. Sinclair.[13] The local press gave a brief history of the founding of the brigade and published a photograph showing some of the

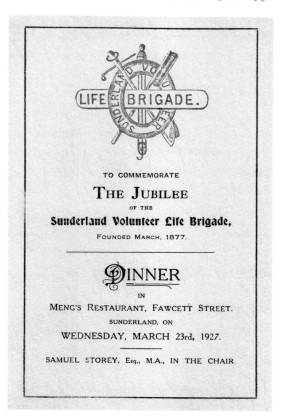

Cover of the menu for the jubilee dinner.

original members with the caption of 'Half Century of Useful and Gallant Work Completed.' Captain John Wilkinson said these words at the dinner:

> To have survived fifty years was no small thing and to have achieved a record of fifty years of untiring and unrewarded service to those who go down to the sea in ships and spend their lives in what is perhaps the most dangerous calling that man had taken was a record of which a Life Brigade might be justly proud.

Between the Wars

The brigade records show that during this period the two brigades continued their training and their work to raise money to fund their service and to purchase equipment. Officers of the brigade were decided upon at each annual meeting and the day-to-day running was managed at monthly committee meetings. Although rescues were less frequent, the volunteers kept up their skills by doing regular instruction drills and by taking part in competitions with other brigades.

A group of original members of Sunderland Volunteer Life Brigade.

HMS *Sentinel* aground on Seaburn Beach, 1923.

Sunderland Lifeboat Crew, *c.*1924. (By kind permission of Sunderland Antiquarian Society)

The *Efos* stranded at Roker, 1927.

HMS *Sentinel*

Sentinel was an obsolete cruiser that had been purchased for breaking up. On 13 February 1923 she was under tow when the line parted due to heavy seas and she ran ashore at Seaburn about 20yds from Whitburn Road, close to the promenade. Sunderland VLB attended but could not get a line on board due to the very high winds. The six crew members were taken off by lifeboat.[14]

Efos

The *Efos* was bound from London on 22 November 1927, travelling up the east coast in a strong easterly gale. Overnight the storm intensified and the vessel had just got round Roker Pier when a huge sea struck her and the waves washed over her decks. She refused to answer to her helm and with the sea breaking over her and driving her stern round she ran ashore. The Roker VLB were called out and they made a number of unsuccessful attempts to get a line on board. The Sunderland lifeboat attended, going out in the terrible seas, but could not get to the lee side due to the rocks; they had to return to port. The captain reported that it was the worst seas that he had ever seen in the harbour.

The brigade fired another line and this time it successfully reached the *Efos* and was secured by the crew. Working in the stormy conditions and in darkness, the brigade brought the crew of seventeen men off one by one; most of the men were from Sunderland. Captain Forsyth, a native of South Shields, was the last to leave the ship. The crew were taken to the brigade watch house and given dry clothing and hot drinks.

Captain Wellburn of the brigade went knocking on the doors of local people to get food for the crew, probably as there would not have been enough supplies for so many men. A Mr Henry of Roker Terrace gave bread and a shopkeeper in St George's Terrace opened up to donate food. The *Sunderland Daily Echo* reported:

> There can be nothing but praise for the work of the Roker Volunteer Life Brigade. They worked with a will and performed their arduous task as if on a drill parade, so orderly and methodically were the duties of each member…[15]

Montagu Seed

This Sunderland-built vessel went aground on the evening of 5 December 1929 after a tow rope broke when she was being towed into harbour. Captain Taylor ordered his vessel to be flooded so that she would ground, otherwise she would have been lost. She was being violently thrown onto the breakwater and was thumping on the bottom with such severity that her crew could not keep their feet. She was holed near the bows. The brigade was on stand-by but a rescue was not required. The vessel was taken off by tugs on the tide and moored at Austin's pontoon. It was commented in the local press that the way in which the vessel withstood the elements and was not more seriously damaged was clear evidence of the excellence of Wear-built ships.[16]

Rescue work by brigadesmen was not confined to official call outs. There is a record in 1935 of the heroic efforts made by two men who rescued a child who had fallen into the River Wear.

Captain Thomas Keenan and brigadesman Wharton had been at the Southside Watch House following a competition. As they walked along they heard a cry and in the water, near the ferryboat landing, was a child struggling. Captain Keenan immediately dived in fully clothed to rescue the child. He was hampered by his heavy clothing but reached the child and, with Wharton's help, they got to the quayside. No further details of the child could be found but he or she certainly had a lucky escape.

Birtley

On 5 May 1936 the *Birtley* was on a voyage from Rotterdam to the Tyne in ballast when, in dense fog, she ran onto rocks north of Whitburn Steel and ended up just yards away from a cornfield. An eyewitness, George Bulmer, stated that he heard loud blasts from a foghorn and then saw the vessel bumping onto the rocks. Despite putting the engines at full speed astern the ship became fast by the bows.

The Whitburn Lifesaving Company tried to use their apparatus to reach the *Birtley* but were unable to do so. The station officer of the coastguard called out the Roker VLB who got a line on board, but the crew decided to stay on board so the brigade stood by all night in case the situation worsened and the crew had to be taken off.

At 3.00 a.m. tugs attempted to pull her off but were unsuccessful. A further attempt was made a few days later by larger tugs but again they failed. It was to be eight months, in early December, before she was finally refloated.[17] The rocks she was settled on had to be blasted away to release her.

The area around the Tyne was a bad one for the *Birtley*. In January 1941 she went aground again, this time on the Long Sands off Tynemouth and again she was refloated. She ended her days in September that year when she broke her back after detonating a mine and sank ten miles off Cromer with the loss of three of her crew.

The VLB continued to play a role in the life and events of Sunderland. In August 1930 the Sunderland South brigade took part in the carnival held in the east end of Sunderland. They put together a tableau with a small version of the lifesaving apparatus and they were awarded second prize. In July 1936 a visit was made to the town by the then Prince of Wales to lay a foundation stone for a new hospital. The brigadesmen formed a guard of honour for the visit and were inspected by the Prince.

The Second World War

It is known that the Roker Watch House, in its prime position overlooking the harbour, was requisitioned by the Royal Navy in early 1939, with them using the lookout and keeping watches. The management committee of the brigade applied to the navy later to try to get some payment for the use of the house, especially as it seems it was not very clean and tidy when the navy left. During these years the men did not just have the often appalling weather conditions to deal with, but the defences against invasion from the sea meant that they had to find their way through these, often at great personal risk.

The Sunderland Volunteer Life Brigade forming a guard of honour for the Prince of Wales' visit, 1936.

Benjamin Robinson receiving the Long Service Medal. (By kind permission of *Sunderland Echo*)

A number of rescues by the brigade are recorded during the war years with a total of 368 lives saved – these were reported on to the committee by the then honorary secretary Benjamin Robinson.

Jellicoe Rose

On 2 February 1940 a wild north-easterly gale was blowing and it was a pitch-black night, raining hard while the brigadesmen were on watch. They then received orders to go to a wreck which was ashore north-east of Roker Pier on the rocks. They arrived on the scene at 7.00 p.m. and took up position on the pier, which was being pounded by heavy seas with waves coming over the top. The brigadesmen had to go down onto the rocks below the pier in order to fire the rocket over the ship.

It was rough underfoot and later the men said that they had got very wet from the spray and from falling into holes. They had to carry the rocket apparatus and, in getting it over the rocks, one of the legs of the gear was broken and they had to improvise by using a piece of stick. Two rockets were fired, a line put on board and the breeches buoy sent over to the vessel. Having done this the crew were unwilling to leave and so they stood by till daylight broke. All of this was, of course, done in the dark as blackout restrictions had to be observed.

In the morning the storm was then going down and the crew decided to stay aboard, so the brigadesmen left the gear set up and some men on watch and went back to the watch house to keep a look out. In the afternoon, about 3.00 p.m., the brigadesmen saw a small boat leave the wreck so they went down to the beach and helped fifteen men ashore. They were all taken to the watch house and given a hot meal; they would later be taken to the Missions to Seamen. The men went back, collected the apparatus and returned to the watch house. Taking part in this rescue were eighteen brigadesmen under the command of Captains N. Wharton, F. Albion, and B. Robinson.

HMS *Fame* and HMS *Ashanti*

In the early hours on 17 October 1940, a flotilla of destroyers were making their way up the east coast to the Tyne from where they were to escort a new battleship HMS *King George V*. At the time, visibility was poor due to heavy drizzle and the darkness but the sea was calm. At full speed two of these ships, HMS *Fame* and HMS *Ashanti* ran straight onto the rocks near Whitburn. Both became well grounded and the *Fame* caught fire as some of her oil pipes were fractured. The two ships ended up side-by-side on the rocks.

At 5.00 a.m. the brigades were called out and, as they had some distance to travel to the scene, loaded their gear onto a lorry to transport it. They arrived near Whitburn in total darkness and located the ships from the sound of their alarm signals. The brigadesmen then had to unload the gear and, deciding they were too near the cliff edge, they carried it about a quarter of a mile to be in a better position. This took a great deal of effort for the fifteen men who had turned out. The brigadesmen then saw that there were two ships involved and that the *Fame* was on fire. This was obviously going to be a major incident and so assistance was called for from the South Shields VLB, just further up the coast, and from the military stationed nearby.

The usual procedure of firing a rocket to get a line to the ship could not be used because of the leaking oil so a different way had to be found for making communication. The brigadesmen

Above: *Fame* and *Ashanti* stranded at Whitburn, 1940.

Left: The badge of HMS *Ashanti* in the watch house.

decided to take the gear onto the rocks, aware that they were at risk from mines in the area and barbed wire. Battling with the sea, the darkness and spilled fuel oil, they got into a position where a line could be floated down to them from the ship. Two men, Captain Robinson and brigadesman William Burton, waded into the sea and secured the line.

The brigades set to work to get all the gear ready and to put firemen on the *Fame* to fight the fire, which was soon brought under control. At 3.00 p.m. that afternoon the brigades were told that there was to be an attempt to refloat both ships on the rising tide so they had a well-deserved rest. At this point they had been on duty for ten hours with only occasional snacks to keep them going. This was wartime and Sunderland and neighbouring areas were key targets for bombing so the military fixed up Bren guns around the area to defend the rescuers should there be an attack.

By 9.30 p.m, however, it was clear that neither ship could be refloated so the lines were put back on. The weather was worsening and it was felt that one ship was likely to turn over. Again in the darkness, the brigadesmen carried the equipment over the rocks, made contact with the ships and then stood by waiting for the call to action. The captains made the decision to arrange the rescuers in watches, as it was clearly going to be a lengthy rescue. This meant that some could rest, as best they could, in a nearby hut while others kept watch and stood by the gear. At 2.30 a.m. the call came to abandon the ships and the brigades were swiftly back in action. The South Shields brigade took the responsibility for getting apparatus onto the *Fame* while the Sunderland brigades attended to the *Ashanti*.

In all, 272 men were rescued, eighty-six by the South Shields VLB and 186 by Sunderland. This remains the world record for the number of men ever rescued in this way in a single incident. It was near midday by the time the brigade packed up their gear and returned to the watch house; they had been working for thirty-two hours and were exhausted.

The cause of the incident was believed to have been that a black and white marker buoy had been dropped to mark an area cleared by minesweepers, and that the captain of the leading ship, *Fame*, mistook this as the marker for the entrance to the Tyne, hence the reason that the ships were going at full speed. Despite attempts to tow them off the rocks, the two ships were still aground at the end of October, but by early November the *Ashanti* was reported as being refloated and docked in Sunderland.[18]

Many years later a story was recounted relating to this rescue. One of the crew rescued was Chief Petty Officer Jack Miller, a Sunderland lad; his wife and son lived at the naval base at Rosyth. To her surprise, his mother opened the door to her house in Hendon Road to see her son there wearing boots that were too big for him. Jack was based in Sunderland for several months as he was one of the crew who was retained during the salvage operations and repairs to the ships. He sent for his family to join him during his stay. He later rejoined the *Fame* and then sailed with the Atlantic convoys. Jack survived the war and left the navy in 1949.[19]

Cairnglen

Another major rescue took place just a few days later. The SS *Cairnglen* was nearing the end of a long and dangerous voyage from Montreal, via Leith, to the Tyne with a cargo of butter, bacon, wheat, engines and tyres. It was Monday 21 October 1940 and there was a gale blowing from the south-east. The ship was at slow speed ahead, and on sighting a black and white buoy

Presentation of the British Empire Medal to William Burton. (By kind permission of *Sunderland Echo*)

The *Marjory M. Hastie.*

the captain gave a new course that should have taken her up the Tyne. What he had seen, however, was the buoy that marked the southern limit of a swept channel that ran up the coast; the ship was almost a mile too far south.

She ran straight onto a reef close to Camel Island at Marsden and ground to a halt. Her plates were ripped for almost all of her 401 ft length. No salvage vessels were available at that particular time and although the sea was temporarily calm, by mid afternoon the incoming tide brought with it heavy seas, and as the tide continued to rise the ship drifted towards the shore.

The South Shields, Roker and Sunderland VLBs were called to the rescue. Captain Robinson of the Roker VLB telephoned the brigadesmen's various places of work to call them out. The gear was loaded onto a wagon and they made their way to Souter Point, the most northerly spot of their area. They could not locate the ship and had to go further north before she was spotted. The gear then had to be carried over ploughed fields to the cliff top. They then stood by as there was to be an attempt to refloat her at about 7.00 p.m.

As this was tried there was a terrible noise and the ship sounded the distress signal. Without any delay, the rocket that had been kept in readiness was fired and went over the fore end but, as the ship was splitting in two, the crew could not get to it. A second rocket was then sent over the stern and communication made with the crew. As this was happening, the brigadesmen spotted a boat being lowered from the stern. Captain Robinson and six men were detailed to assist the men in the boat while the others managed the apparatus. They had to go through the barbed wire and scramble down the cliffs, risking any land mines, to show the boat where to land. The boat overturned just as it reached the shore and, after a struggle, sixteen crew men were helped up the cliff face.

Meanwhile, the rocket apparatus was being used to bring thirty-five men from the ship. Word was sent across to say that there was a sick man aboard and a volunteer was needed to go over to the ship to assist. All there offered to go but William Burton was selected and he later received the British Empire Medal for his services. In all, fifty-one people were rescued from the *Cairnglen*. The brigade was in attendance for about twenty-two hours and were very wet and cold, but thankful that no one had been lost.

Marjory M. Hastie

During one of the worst snowstorms in the north-east of England for half a century, the Sunderland VLB was called out to a minesweeper that had struck a mine and then been washed ashore onto rocks at Marsden in the north of the brigade's area. It was 8.00 a.m. on 20 February 1941 when the call came and, as was the procedure at the time, the police assisted in calling out the brigadesmen. A motor lorry was to be used to carry the gear, and twice on the way to the watch house it became stuck in the snow. Captains Wharton and Robinson, with twelve brigadesmen, eventually got underway but twice they had to get out and dig the lorry free from the snowdrifts.

On arrival they set up their gear and fired a rocket which went over the ship, but in sending over the gear the whip line (which carries the breeches buoy) became fouled. The time taken to pull in the line and fire another rocket would have meant a delay so Captain Robinson plunged into the icy sea and released the line. He had to be helped ashore as he was overcome with the cold. Twenty-two crewmen were taken off the vessel to safety. While this was happening, another brigadesman, Thomas Thirlwell, collapsed from exposure and had to be taken to hospital.

Camroux I

There had been a thick snow squall all night when, at daylight on 6 March 1942, there was word to call the brigade to a vessel on the rocks off the fishermens' cottages, Whitburn. The brigadesmen left the watch house at 7.30 a.m. in a snowstorm and found the ship about 350yds off shore: it was the *Camroux I*. A line was put aboard and, with the help of some soldiers from the battery stationed there, nine men were rescued. The brigadesmen noted that it was an extremely cold night, especially on the bleak shore, with the wind from the north-east blowing half a gale. The men got back to the watch house at midnight.

In Memoriam

Many men who served with the brigade also served in the armed forces during military conflicts, but there is no full record of those who gave their lives for their country. There is, however, one special memorial in the watch house that commemorates two Sunderland VLB brothers who lost their lives in action during the Second World War.

Alfred John Fenton was born on 1 February 1916, the son of Matthew and Mary Ann Fenton of Monkwearmouth. He enrolled as a brigade member on 4 February 1937 and served with the Roker brigade. He enrolled as a gunner in the Royal Artillery and was killed on 2 May 1942 whilst serving overseas. His body lies in Takoradi cemetery in Ghana.[20]

Alfred Fenton.

James Fenton.

Above: Takoradi cemetery. (By kind
permission of The War Graves
Photographic Project)

Right: Lowestoft Naval Memorial. (By
kind permission of The War Graves
Photographic Project)

1943 LIEUTENANT	1943 LEADING SEAMAN	1943 SEAMAN
BOYD W. H.	CHALMERS J. W.	DOCHERTY J.
CHILDS J. N.	COSTELLO W.	DONLAN A.
CROSBY J. R.	DAWSON G. J.	DORES A. H.
DAVIS L. E.	DODD T. J.	DOW W.
FRADGLEY J. R.	EMSLEY W.	DRYBURGH G.
HAVERCROFT E.	FIRTH M. V.	DYE E. H.
ROPER D. R. V.	FYFE P.	ELLIS J.
SUB LIEUTENANT	HARVEY G. M.	FENTON J. B. R.
BAKER A. W. J.	HEARD P.	FINLAY W. A.
CARTER R. S.	JASPER E. S.	FRANKISH J.
CRAWSHAW J.	MATHESON N.	GARNER J. L.
HARRIS R. B.	PEARCE C. R.	GOODING W.
NEVE F. P. W.	PYNE G. E.	GRAINGER W. M.
ACT. SUB LIEUTENANT	RICHARDSON W. E.	GRANT L.
LACEY K. D. F.	TAYLOR J. D.	GRIFFITHS W. T.
	WILKINSON T.	GULLY R. A.
SKIPPER LIEUTENANT	WINDLE J. W.	HARVEY A. E. C.
BLOCKWELL F. G.	WINSPEAR W. T.	HARVEY C. W.
EVERETT J. L.	WYLIE J. E. R.	HENDERSON A. S.
WHICHELLO G. A.		HERD S.
	SEAMAN	HOPEWELL G. H.
SKIPPER	ABBOTTS H.	HOWLAND W. J. E.
BROWN C.	ALEXANDER E. D.	HUGHES R. E.
CONNOLLY W. J.	ALLEN A. L.	HUGHES W. J.
GEDDES G. G.	BARCOCK E.	HUNTER W.
JAPPY A.	BARKER G. E. W.	JONES S.
NICHOLSON J. W.	BARNSTON S. G. J.	LAMBERT G. M.
NOBLE J. H.	BIRD J.	LANGFORD R.
SALENIUS S.	BLACK C. L.	LARDER C. G.
SMITH G. A. S.	BLACKWELL H. R.	LEES J. S.
SOANES A. A.	BLADES A. R.	LEWIS D. R. D.
TEMPLE E. W.	BRIDGE H.	LOCKERBIE J. A.
	BROTHERTON G. E.	LYON B. O.
SECOND HAND	BROWN L. J.	McCRORIE H. M.
EDWARDS W.	BUCKMASTER J. H.	McDONALD R.
GLENTWORTH H.	BUDDO J.	McHUGH A. L.
GOVIS W.	CARTER J. S.	McKINNON R.
HOOKEM E.	CHAPMAN G. A.	MacDERMID D. A.
INNES J. S.	CHESWORTH R.	MACDONALD A.
LOWRIE R.	CHILDS A. H.	MacDONALD D.
MURRAY A. G.	COLBOURNE R. M.	MacKENZIE J.
OLDMAN W. J. D.	COLEMAN P.	MACLEAN A.
PATTERSON A. W.	CONNOLLY J.	MacLEOD M.
STANSFIELD C. W.	COOK F. W.	MARTIN A.
WILEMAN S. A.	COWELL M. W.	MARTIN W.
WILSON W. H.	COWIE I.	MASON H.
	COX C. W.	MEADS T.
PETTY OFFICER	CRABTREE G.	MILNE P.
SAYERS A. A. B.	CRAIG J.	MOULDS M.
	CRAIG R.	MULVANEY G. N.
LEADING SEAMAN	CURPHEY K.	NASH N. J.
CAMBURN E.	CURTIS S. C.	NEWSON J. C.
	DAVIDSON J.	NORTON H.
	DELL D. W.	OWEN J.

Plaque on the naval memorial showing James Fenton's name. (By kind permission of The War Graves Photographic Project)

James Broomfield Robinson Fenton was Alfred's older brother, being born on 7 February 1913. He enrolled in the Roker brigade with his brother on the same date. James was a seaman and he served in the Royal Naval Patrol Service safeguarding the British coast. He served on board HM Trawler *Franc Tireur*, a ship that had been taken over by the Admiralty in 1941 and converted for minesweeping. On 25 September 1943 the vessel was torpedoed and sunk by the German motor torpedo boat S-96 off Harwich, England. James died along with his thirteen crewmates. He is commemorated on the Lowestoft Naval Memorial in Suffolk along with almost 2,400 others from this service.[21]

Notes

1 *Sunderland Daily Echo*, 12 November 1901, p.6
2 Ibid.
3 *Sunderland Daily Echo*, 13 November 1901, p.3
4 *Sunderland Daily Echo*, 12 November 1901, p.6
5 *Sunderland Daily Echo*, 13 November 1901, p.3
6 *Sunderland Daily Echo*, 14 November 1901, p.6
7 *Sunderland Daily Echo*, 22 November 1904, p.6
8 *Sunderland Daily Echo*, 5 January 1905, p.3
9 *Sunderland Daily Echo*, 24 January 1913, p.8
10 Ex inf John Dale
11 *Sunderland Daily Echo*, 6 December 1915, p.6
12 *Sunderland Daily Echo*, 31 October 1919, p.4
13 *Sunderland Daily Echo*, 24 March 1927, p.7
14 *Sunderland Daily Echo*, 13 February 1923, p.5
15 *Sunderland Daily Echo*, 21 November 1927, p.5
16 *Sunderland Daily Echo*, 6 December 1929, p.9
17 *Sunderland Daily Echo*, 5 May 1946, p.1
18 National Archive CAB 66/13/15
19 *Sunderland Echo*, 23 February 1988, p.7
20 Commonwealth War Graves Commission, www.cwgc.org
21 Ibid.

seven

TIMES OF CHANGE 1950–1990

The Closure of the Sunderland South Brigade

The two brigades at Sunderland worked separately, but alongside each other, until the late 1950s. At times they came together with regard to fundraising and for special events, and sometimes they worked jointly in a rescue. The loss of records from the Sunderland South brigade means that there is a lack of detailed information on the reasons for its closure, so reliance has had to be placed on the records of the Roker brigade, which give few facts. The annual general meeting of the Roker brigade on 19 July 1957 refers to four members of the Sunderland South going over to Roker and records the possibility of the Sunderland South being defunct, although no reasons are given for this. The divisional inspector of HM Coastguard wrote to both brigades in March that year suggesting that the two be merged.

A meeting at the Roker Watch House on 6 December 1957 records that a letter had been received from Sunderland South stating that they intended to wind-up their affairs and would arrange for the transfer of their members to the Roker brigade. The members of the Sunderland South brigade finally closed the door of their watch house on New Year's Eve 1957. After over eighty years, the southern coast of Sunderland no longer had its own dedicated shore-based rescue service. Many of the items that had been on display were moved to the Roker Watch House where they can still be viewed.

The Roker brigade then took over the responsibility for both sides of the River Wear, its harbour and the surrounding coastline. It continued to be based at the Roker Watch House and to train the volunteers in the use of the lifesaving apparatus. At the annual meeting in 1959, the decision was made to change its name and it became known as the Sunderland VLB. It was to be some years though before the brigade had the opportunity to put their skills into practice again.

Sunderland Brigade, 1946.

Janet

The brigade was sometimes summoned to an incident even though they were not called upon to use the rocket apparatus. They could be on stand-by in case they were needed, or be providing support to other services. In October 1960 three fishermen were on the *Janet* when the engine broke down. They set off flares that were seen on shore, and though the lifeboat and brigade were called, the lifeboat could not get near to the vessel. Lines were thrown to the men who were then pulled to safety.[1]

As well as the regular drills and watch-keeping on the coast, the brigadesmen continued with fundraising efforts and regularly took their place in competitions which were held between different brigades. There were three trophies that were competed for – the Chronicle Cup, the Wear Ship-Owners Shield and the Elizabethan Cup.

The Chronicle Cup and the Wearside Ship-Owners Shield were set up in the 1920s and the Elizabethan Cup in 1962. The Chronicle Cup was awarded by the *Newcastle Chronicle* in 1921 and was competed for by VLBs and auxiliary coastguard teams from the north-east; it tested the efficiency and speed with which the brigadesmen could set up their apparatus, aiming for the 'perfect' drill. All the teams trained long and hard beforehand as the pride of their brigade was at stake. The teams had to set up the breeches buoy apparatus as if a rescue had just taken place and then, on a command, they would stow the gear and return it to a base. A member of the coastguard acted as umpire and went over the actions in detail. As there was usually little to choose between the teams, a 'complication' was put in by the umpire. This may have been that a line had broken or a tripod leg had snapped. The captains would then have to decide how to get around the problem and instruct their team.

Setting up the rocket launcher.

Rocket apparatus drill with rocket in launcher.

Sunderland Volunteer Life Brigade with Ship-Owners Shield. (By kind permission of *Sunderland Echo*)

The Elizabethan Trophy was awarded to the brigade who had completed the four best quarterly drills in a year. It was presented for competition by Mr Tommy Simpson, a member of Tynemouth VLB who served in that brigade for seventy years.

The Wear Ship-Owners Shield was first competed for in 1929 and took place annually between the Tynemouth, South Shields and Sunderland Brigades. This was a timed competition judging the speed at which the brigades could set up the equipment to carry out a rescue and stow the apparatus. It was held at each brigade's training ground in turn with the home team providing refreshments for all.

The judges for the competition were drawn from all the brigades and their deliberations often went on long after the competition ended. On one occasion they took so long that the teams had all gone home before they reached a verdict. Brigade members who took part in the competitions recollect the intense rivalry between the teams and the excitement of competing. In 1971, Sunderland VLB won all three trophies for the first time in their history.

Sunderland VLB with the three trophies, 1971. (By kind permission of *Sunderland Echo*)

The Last Breeches Buoy Rescue – *Adelfotis II*

The last breeches buoy rescue by Sunderland VLB took place during a terrible storm on Sunday 20 January 1963 when the Lebanese registered steamer *Adelfotis II*, captained by Nicolas Leonardis, ran aground at South Shields North Foreshore in a force 9 gale. The ship was running for shelter in the Tyne and the weather was too bad to take a pilot on board. She struck the Black Midden rocks, the scene of many a shipwreck, and then rebounded and was swept across the harbour grounding at Herd Sands.

The huge waves drove her 300yds along the sands in the following few hours. In danger of capsizing, and with tugs and lifeboats unable to get near, the mayday call sent out by the Greek crew was answered by both the South Shields and Sunderland VLBs. A line was fired to the ship and within two hours all of the twenty-three crew members, and the ship's mascot, one small dog, were rescued. It was a very difficult rescue due to the weather conditions, which had not eased.

Some brigadesmen had to act as human anchors to the equipment to prevent it being blown out of the ground. Some went into the waves tied to safety lines, when the conditions meant that the lines and breeches buoy became submerged, to pull the crew to the shore. The crew were immersed in the sea whilst being taken off by breeches buoy and were treated for exposure. Luckily, none of them suffered any serious injuries, but the dog, Manuela, had to be returned to Greece due to quarantine laws and she was escorted to another ship, bound for Athens, by the River Tyne police. Part of the rescue was captured on television newsreel and it clearly shows the terrible conditions under which the rescuers worked and the gratefulness of the crew when they were landed.

The beached *Adelfotis II* was a draw to the public and it was agreed by the two brigades that there was an opportunity to use the wreck for publicity for much-needed recruits. On a cold but calm 23 February, a public re-enactment of the rescue took place and drew large crowds. The brigades used the rocket equipment and each took off two 'survivors' by breeches buoy, volunteers from a local Sea Scout troop.

The brigade continued to train with the rocket apparatus and stand in readiness at times of bad weather, but there were no more calls from the coastguard to attend a rescue. Many VLBs and lifesaving companies around the country had closed down and, when the rocket apparatus became obsolete, there was little reason for most to keep going. The Sunderland brigade, along with those at Tynemouth and South Shields, changed the focus of their work to be able to continue in active support of the coastguard and lifeboats and to provide lifesaving services.

The brigade was called out on other occasions after this but the rescue equipment was not needed. In July 1966 they attended an incident when two yachtsmen were stranded after their vessel fouled a fishing net off the Toll Bar at Ryhope. There was a possibility that the *Sirius* could be driven onto the rocks, so the brigade stood by until the men were rescued by the Seaham lifeboat.

Adelfotis II rescue, 1963.

Adelfotis II aground at South
Shields.

The Sunderland Volunteer Life
Brigade Land Rover.

Centenary 1977

The Sunderland VLB celebrated the centenary of its founding with a dinner dance held on 19 March 1977. Guests were invited from the local council, HM Coastguard and other brigades.

As part of the celebrations, a demonstration drill was staged using the breeches buoy between the north and south piers. The centenary was also celebrated with a floral display done by Sunderland council staff at Roker Park. A special badge was struck to commemorate the centenary.

The 1980s saw progressive changes as the appropriateness of the breeches buoy and rocket equipment was questioned by central government because of the decline in its use. In 1983 the three existing brigades successfully resisted an attempt to close them down, but they became responsible for the provision of all equipment apart from rescue rockets and flares. A few years later, in March 1987, the Government decided to stop the supply of rockets and flares.[2] The three existing brigades of Tynemouth, South Shields and Sunderland agreed a joint approach be made to HM Coastguard and the decision was rescinded while discussions took place with the brigades.

The reprieve was short lived as, in 1988, central government disbanded the use of breeches buoy equipment and the withdrawal of the equipment was announced by the then transport minister Paul Channon. He said that the improvement in the provision of helicopters and lifeboats meant that the use of the breeches buoy had progressively declined. Indeed, the Sunderland VLB had last used the equipment in 1963 but remained trained and ready to use it at any time. The news was treated with dismay and objections, with brigadesmen stating that there were times when lifeboats and helicopters could not reach a stranded ship.

Although there was no longer the opportunity to do breeches buoy rescues, the brigade wanted to continue the service of saving lives, and so members completed the necessary training to undertake cliff rescues. New equipment was needed and fundraising took place to achieve this. During this period the brigade also became more up-to-date in the way they transported their equipment. In 1985 a second-hand Land Rover was purchased and it was kitted out with the colours used on HM Coastguard vehicles and the brigade logo. It was also fitted with a winch and a radio transmitter/receiver. The inside was modified to carry team members and their rescue equipment.

Fundraising went ahead to cover the costs of insurance and road tax. Permission was given by the police for the vehicle to be fitted with a blue flashing light. The rocket cart house was cleared out to garage the new vehicle. HM Coastguard gave the Land Rover the call-sign 'Roker Mobile'. The vehicle was sponsored by the *Sunderland Echo* for a year and the sum of £200 presented to cover the tax and insurance.[3] The Land Rover was replaced twice with similar vehicles, and these served the brigade until 2008 when funding was raised to enable the purchase of a Ford Ranger.

Sunderland brigade continued with its work during this period, often assisting other emergency services in rescues and searches. The calls to the brigade were very varied and many requested assistance with searches when a person or child had gone missing, or someone had been washed into the sea during a storm.

In June 1985 the brigade assisted in the rescue of a youth from cliffs at Ryhope, and in September that year they received a request to attend a scene near Ryhope where a car had gone over the cliff. The brigade team formed part of a full-scale search, which involved the police and helicopters, for the driver of the vehicle who must have been hurt. The car had been stolen and a man had been seen leaving the wreck, but despite an extensive search he was not found.[4]

Menu cover for centenary dinner

In 1988 there were two call outs; in May two eleven year olds were seen on the cliffs at Ryhope. They had been trapped by the incoming tide and had climbed about 120ft up the cliff before getting stuck on a ledge. Luckily they were spotted by two youths who raised the alarm. The brigade was called out along with other emergency services and attended the scene to assist. A police officer swam to the bottom of the cliff and climbed up to reassure them, meanwhile ropes were lowered to lift them to the cliff top. After a check-up both were allowed home.[5]

In June the brigade responded to a report of a person and a dog being in the sea. The brigade attended along with other emergency services to undertake a search. The man was found safe, but after a search the body of the dog was recovered.

On occasions, despite the best efforts of all the emergency services, a tragedy occurs. In February 1990 a young girl was swept into the sea at Seaburn by a huge wave. Onlookers made several attempts to rescue her in very difficult conditions. The brigade joined a large search effort to find the girl that covered a large coastal area. Tragically, her body was found a few hours later.

Other searches that year included assisting a sailing dinghy that got into difficulties at Roker Pier and joining a search for the occupants when a rubber dinghy was found on Roker beach; in this case it was found that no one was missing.

Notes

1 *Sunderland Echo*, 24 October 1960, p.6
2 *Sunderland Echo*, 4 March 1987, p.10
3 *Sunderland Echo*, 22 April 1986, p.6
4 *Sunderland Echo*, 30 September 1985, p.1
5 *Sunderland Echo*, 16 May 1988, p.1

eight

THE MODERN
SUNDERLAND VLB

Sunderland VLB, along with its fellow brigades at Tynemouth and South Shields, has survived because it adapted to doing other work after the rocket and breeches buoy equipment became obsolete in the 1980s. A declared facility for HM Coastguard, the brigade works with other emergency services in continuing its history of saving life and also in observation of the coastal area and keeping a visual watch of the shore.

Being adaptable to change, and prepared to train with new equipment, the brigade further adjusted by eventually accepting women as members. Although women had always had a key supporting role, particularly in relation to fundraising and social events, they could not be full members of the brigade. Rose Roberts, wife of a deputy captain, became the brigade's secretary in 1993 and the first female member of the brigade.

Now men and women serve together equally in all areas of the brigade's work, including the search and rescue team. There are four main areas to the work of the brigade: search and rescue, coastwatch, the museum and fundraising. All of these are equally important, but each has a different focus, although fundraising crosses the other three elements.

Search and Rescue

The search and rescue team is fully trained in search methods and rescue techniques, including equipment for cliff rescues. The team answers a wide variety of requests for assistance, being called upon by HM Coastguard in times of need. The team works very closely with HM Coastguard, the RNLI, the police and other rescue services, including RAF helicopters, providing assistance and support in many ways. The call outs can be varied and although some turn out to be false alarms, mostly with good intent, none can be ignored.

On 13 February 1994 a storm was blowing and high waves began to wash over Sunderland's north pier. The conditions had been fine earlier and people had gone on to the pier, some of them to fish. Two teenage boys were playing by dodging the waves when a huge wall of water fell over the pier, knocking them down, and threatened to wash them into the sea. A local

Above: Training with Royal Air Force Boulmer.

Right: Rose Roberts, the first female member of the brigade.

Sunderland Volunteer Life Brigade members outside the watch house.

Cliff training near Souter Point, Whitburn.

Training with the Royal National Lifeboat Institution.

Setting up apparatus for cliff rescue.

fisherman had been getting ready to leave the pier because of the worsening conditions when he saw that one of the boys was trapped against the railing while the other was being washed down towards the end of the pier. He grabbed the boy in danger of being washed into the sea and pulled him to some shelter at the pier end; he then went back for the other boy.

Meanwhile, the incident had been spotted at the brigade's watch house and they alerted the coastguard before hurrying to the scene .The conditions were so bad that an RAF helicopter was called to airlift the two boys to hospital. Marine police, coastguards and brigadesmen braved the conditions to get onto the pier to escort off about thirty people who were stranded. The brigadesmen and coastguards then went back onto the pier until the two boys were airlifted off. They then had to leave the pier through a tunnel that runs underneath its length. This tunnel was built so that lighthouse keepers could get to the lighthouse in any weather conditions.

In December 1998, the Sunderland VLB along with HM Coastguard, the RNLI and RAF and police helicopters assisted in the rescue of a man from the sea near Hendon. He was eventually winched to safety and treated in hospital. Children and young people often do not realise the dangers of climbing on or near cliffs and this was the case when a young boy had to be rescued from rocks at Roker. He had fallen and his foot became wedged in the rocks, trapping him for about twenty minutes. The VLB and HM Coastguard attended and paramedics were called to treat him, with the brigade keeping an eye on the rising tide while the rescue took place.

The year 2002 also saw a rescue from the north pier when sixty people had to be evacuated. It was Sunday 3 November and many people were enjoying using the pier when a sudden change in the weather brought 14ft-high waves crashing over it. The lifeboat was called out and attended along with Sunderland VLB and Seaham coastguard. The lifeboat stood by the pier throughout the operation in case anyone was swept into the sea. The members of the public were instructed to start leaving the pier as it was considered very risky to try to get them onto

125th anniversary badge.

125th anniversary cake.

the boat. With Humber coastguard co-ordinating the communications, the services all worked together until all the people were safely on the shore.[1]

The brigade is on call every day of the year, and in 2002 there was a call out on Christmas Day after reports of a vessel on fire at sea. Despite a thorough search nothing was found. 2002 was also the year of the 125th anniversary of the founding of SVLB. A special badge was commissioned to celebrate this achievement and good wishes were sent from other institutions.

The year 2003 saw a number of call outs to searches where the brigade worked alongside other services. In April, two children went missing and the search and rescue team carried out a search along with the coastguards and a police helicopter. They were found a short distance away, safe and well. The brigade was also asked to assist South Shields VLB in manning a helicopter landing site after a body had been retrieved from the rocks at Lizard Point. The following month the call was to search for a fisherman missing from a capsized boat. After six and a half hours the teams were stood down as nothing had been found.

August brought a major search at Seaham after reports of a person on the rocks but, despite an intensive search, no trace was found. They also attended to provide safety advice to people using the coastal area; prevention of accidents is always better than an accident occurring. These call outs included warning children of playing on a pipe when the tide was coming in and advice to a jet-skier after complaints that he was outside the designated area. In all there were twenty-three call outs during the year to a wide variety of incidents.

While patrolling the seafront during a wild afternoon in February 2004, the team saw people 'wave dodging' – running through the very high waves washing over the promenade. Several people have been washed to their deaths in the area in such circumstances. The team positioned the Land Rover so they could monitor the situation and were so concerned that they went on foot patrol to warn people of the dangers. They had to warn many people who seemed oblivious to the great danger of the strength of the waves. They eventually returned to the watch house, drenched through, after nearly two hours.

Rescue team members need a good head for heights.

In April, Sunderland VLB joined their fellow brigade members of South Shields to assist in a search after an emergency flare had been sighted off the coast. With the Tynemouth lifeboat launched for a sea search, the volunteers scanned the coastline from South Shields Pier to Whitburn. Nothing was found but the team had played their part in ensuring that no one was in danger. Later that month they assisted in the rescue of a harbour porpoise which had come ashore on Roker beach; unfortunately it did not survive.

The evening of 7 July was very busy. The search and rescue team had just completed a cliff exercise near Marsden when one member sighted two red distress flares. While on their way to investigate this incident, the team were asked to attend another incident of red flares being sited, this time over the River Tyne; Sunderland coastguard attended the Marsden incident. Sunderland VLB joined colleagues from Tynemouth VLB in this search along the river entrance and foreshore; nothing was found and the team returned to Sunderland.

In the meantime, a search was underway near South Shields for a group of young people who had been seen swimming and who were possibly in difficulties. South Shields VLB and coastguards, along with an RAF helicopter, were undertaking this incident. At the scene it was found that one young person had left the area and a description was circulated. While on their way home to South Shields, two members of the Sunderland brigade spotted a person who they thought was the missing swimmer. They stopped and stayed with her until coastguard personnel arrived and escorted her back for medical checks. All three young people were airlifted to hospital with possible hypothermia.

There were a total of forty-three call outs in 2004. These included providing first aid to a man who had dived off the pier, assisting a yacht to get safely into Sunderland harbour and several calls to assist animals in distress.

In March 2005 Sunderland VLB was asked to carry out a search of the Sunderland area for the source of a radio transmission that was blocking the distress channel used by shipping. It is vital that this channel is kept open so that ships' crews and fishermen can quickly call for assistance if they are having problems. A check of Sunderland marina showed that no vessels there were the source of the signal, so the search was widened.

Engineers from the Office of Communications and the Radiocommunications Agency provided some additional details. After many hours of searching by the VLB team, in the early hours of the following morning the signal was finally traced to a ship undergoing repairs that appeared to have a faulty radio. Locating the source of this problem enabled the VLB to clear the distress channel, leaving it free for emergency use.

Occasions do arise when the brigade does not just rescue people. November 2002 saw a call to people who were trapped in a mine shaft at High Spen near Gateshead. On arrival at the scene, the brigade found that it was in fact a horse that was trapped, but of course it was still in need of rescue. The brigade and the coastguards worked to free the horse, which was in a hole

Tracing the source of the radio transmission.

Cycle patrol at the ready.

about two metres deep with only its head, forelegs and part of its chest visible. As it was very distressed, a vet administered a tranquiliser before the operation started. The horse, Storm, was then hauled to safety.

In March 2006 some anglers attempted to retrieve their motor boat from the beach using a car and trailer. Before they could do this the tide turned and the car began to sink. The rescue team attended and managed to haul out the boat but could not pull out the car, which was stuck in the sand. The services of the RNLI tractor were called upon to assist.

In 2006 a proposal was made that the brigade acquire the necessary equipment and training to commence cycle patrols along the seafront. By March 2007 this had gone live and five experienced volunteers had finished training. Essential equipment such as a first aid pack and radios is carried in panniers on the cycles. This service is vital at times when vehicles are not allowed on the main seafront road, such as during the air show and road races, but they can also be used on the promenades at any time. The cycles enable the brigade to respond swiftly to incidents, they are easily seen by the public, can access routes not open to motor vehicles and the volunteers can quickly call on support from other emergency services when the need arises.

Coastwatch

The coastwatch at Sunderland VLB is affiliated to the National Coastwatch Institution (NCI), which is a voluntary organisation set up to keep a visual watch along UK shores. Its purpose is to assist in the protection and preservation of life at sea and around the UK coastline. There are about forty NCI stations which are manned by over 1,700 volunteers keeping watch around the British Isles.

Sunderland Coastwatch was set up in 2005 and officially opened in October that year. Volunteers are fully trained and provide 'eyes and ears' along the coastal area including the harbour, beaches and piers. This visual watch was re-established after many years as, whilst technology and sophisticated systems are aids to improved safety, these cannot spot a distress flare, an overturned boat or a yachtsman or fisherman in trouble. Other activities like diving, body boarding, wind surfing and canoeing are made safer with visual surveillance, and the watch-keepers provide additional safety during events such as the annual Sunderland air show.

The coastwatchers monitor the weather, shipping and activities. The significance of this was made clear when a boat was reported to be on fire off the coast. The Sunderland Coastwatchers were able to report that they had actually logged this vessel returning into the River Wear. This meant that a large and expensive sea and air search was avoided.

In 2008 two coastwatchers on duty spotted a boy who had been surfing in difficulties in the water. They were calling in the incident when a jet-skier saw the boy and went to pick him up. The brigade followed this up by going to the landing point where a decision was made to call an ambulance. The boy was treated for hypothermia and made a full recovery.

As part of its commitment to the involvement and education of young people, the brigade offers training to young people taking part in the Duke of Edinburgh Award scheme in coast watching. The young people cover all the relevant training and learn how to keep watch while being supervised by trained and experienced coastwatch officers.

The view from the coastwatch lookout.

Working with other services at the Sun City Triathlon.

Jon Gifford (right), National Coastwatch Institution Chairman, and Sunderland Volunteer Life Brigade President Graham Hall, 2006.

Coastwatcher on duty in the lookout.

Name board of the *Olivia* on display at the watch house.

The Museum

The VLB watch houses were set up as bases for the volunteers for training, storage of equipment and, in the early days, to accommodate shipwrecked sailors. The last South Side watch house closed in 1958 and the building was demolished some time later. The Roker Watch House, built 1905/6, still fulfils most of the functions that it was built to provide. Over its 130-year history the brigade has amassed and obtained a large number of artefacts, photographs and memorabilia, mainly in relation to the work of the brigade and the rescues.

The Roker Watch House acts as a museum for the brigade and its past, providing a rare insight into this part of Sunderland's maritime history. The walls are covered with the name boards from ships, some of which were salvaged from ships attended by the brigade and others which were made by the brigadesmen themselves as mementos. The earliest shore-based lifesaving is represented by a replica Manby Mortar and the more modern Boxer rockets adorn one of the walls. There are four figureheads from the days of sailing ships, and one of the old woollen ganseys worn by the Roker brigadesmen.

Mast light on display at the watch house.

Figureheads from one of the four ships.

A Wartime Disaster

One brass plaque in the museum has no link to the history of the brigade, but the members are proud to be its custodians. It is a memorial plaque that used to be in the old Sunderland children's hospital and it commemorates a Second World War maritime disaster. In the disaster, seventy-seven evacuee children and six of their escorts died; nine of these children were from Sunderland. The plaque in the watch house gives their names and ages. The children were being evacuated to Canada from many parts of England, which must have been a very difficult decision for their parents.

On 17 September 1940 their ship, the *City of Benares*, was struck by a torpedo from a U-boat. It was just after 10.00 p.m., a cold, dark and stormy night, when the order to 'abandon ship' was given. Most of the passengers got into the lifeboats but there were difficulties in launching some and others got swamped by the sea. Many of the passengers and crew could not survive the awful conditions. A Sunderland girl, Eleanor Wright, was rescued by the crew of HMS *Hurricane* after spending many hours clinging to an upturned boat.[2] One lifeboat was washed away from the others and in it was a Sunderland boy, Billy Short, aged nine years old. It was a week before this lifeboat was found and the people rescued. Billy's younger brother Peter, aged five, died in the disaster.

A bed at the children's hospital was purchased from donations given after the disaster, and the brass plaque was placed above it to commemorate those lost. After the closure of the hospital the plaque was moved to a different site. It was rediscovered when this site closed and eventually was offered to the brigade. The watch house is the only place in Sunderland where these children are permanently remembered.

Irene and Edith Smith, Sunderland sisters who died in the *City of Benares* disaster.

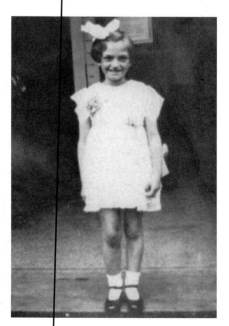

Maureen Dixon also lost her life.

In 2008 the brigade applied for, and was awarded, one of the specially designed flags which marked the handover of the Olympic Games from Beijing to London. All across the country these flags were raised to signal the actual handover in China. Local sports groups were invited to the brigade's watch house and a 'Flying the Flag' ceremony was held when the flag was raised by the then deputy mayor of the city, Councillor Dennis Richardson.

The museum works to keep alive the history of the VLB and promotes educational visits so that young people in the city can learn of the contribution made by the men and women of the VLB in saving lives for over 130 years.

Flying the flag celebration. (By kind permission of *Sunderland Echo*)

Dedication of Sunderland Volunteer Life Brigade kneeler at St Peter's Church, 2008.

Fred Roberts, Senior Captain, with tankard awarded for long service. (By kind permission of *Sunderland Echo*)

The Work Continues

Improvements in available equipment, health and safety legislation and the desire to continually improve the range of services provided mean changes in training and the need to provide additional equipment. In 2008 the brigade became the owner of a new Ford Ranger, to replace the Land Rover, due to the generosity of the Tom Cowie Foundation. The Ranger is fully fitted out to carry the rescue equipment and first aid equipment.

All members are offered first aid training and some have also completed training in the use of automatic defibrillators. The Coastwatch now operates three days a week, and this will be extended when more volunteers are recruited and trained.

Research continues into the history of the brigade, the ships that were assisted and, importantly, into the men who served as part of the brigade over the long years of its service. The museum is improving its information and displays so that the work of Sunderland Volunteer Life Brigade and its members is never forgotten.

Notes
1 *Sunderland Echo*, 5 November 2002, p.2
2 Ralph Barker, *Children of the Benares* (Wirral: Avid Publications 2003)

Ford Ranger being presented by Sir Tom Cowie.

Ford Ranger outside the watch house.